A Compassionate Approach to Addiction Intervention

by Howie M.

as told to

Mary Beth Lagerborg and
G. Dale Meyer, Ph.D.

his ongoing recovery and professional service life of nearly 50 years. Little wonder that Howie has been so widely recognized and respected within the addiction treatment, recovery and intervention professional community!

This short intervention book focuses on the many integral components of effective intervention work with alcoholic and chemically dependent persons. Howie has delineated the interventionist's most crucial and essential ingredients in the process of successful intervention work. The cornerstones of his intervention model include understanding, empathy and compassion, respect and dignity, sensitivity, and extensive knowledge and experience pertaining to the internal, cognitive, behavioral, and interpersonal world of the addict. This book will be an excellent training tool and resource for all addiction professionals who are desirous of developing and/or enhancing their professional skill set in this particular area. I also think that all of us who have devoted our lives and professional careers to the addiction treatment field will find this book to be inspiring and meaningful in numerous ways. Howie openly and unflinchingly explores all facets of the intervention process: interventions that went well, but ones that failed...the great outcomes, but also the struggles, tragedies, risks and multifaceted realities of not just the addiction treatment and recovery field, but all contemporary health care workers and enterprises.

I am grateful simply to be able to refer to Howie and his wife Pat as friends over all these years, and I also especially recommend this book for addiction treatment providers.

Gary G. Forrest, Ed.D., Ph.D.
Licensed Clinical Psychologist and
Executive Director, Psychotherapy Associates, PC
Colorado Springs, CO

[I consider Howie] my best friend, mentor, spiritual advisor, colleague, surrogate father, an unconditionally loving human being, and partner in sobriety and in interventions. "Mara," he used to say, "I must pass on this knowledge and passion to you and to others while I still can. We must keep helping the alcoholic/addict, because for each one we touch, we also touch the lives of their children, their children's children, and on and on from there...."

Mara Lehnert, CACIII
Certified Intervention Trainer and Interventionist

In 1985 I moved from Nebraska to Colorado to work for a treatment center. There I met Howie. He had a reputation for being a kind and caring man. I found Howie to be one of those special people that others tend to gravitate towards. As our friendship grew he became my mentor, and I have had the privilege of not only working with him but also observing how he has worked with others. He helped me be a better husband, a better father, a better grandfather, a better counselor, and, I believe, a better man.

My wife and I have become close to Howie and Pat and consider them our closest friends. We have enjoyed many wonderful times together. I know many people who are clean and sober today and their journey began with Howie suggesting they could have a better life.

A few years ago I came across a writing by Sam Shoemaker, an Episcopalian priest who was associated with The Oxford Groups in New York City. He was a spiritual advisor to Bill Wilson and Dr. Robert Smith, better known as Dr. Bob, the founders of Alcoholics Anonymous. It was entitled "I Stand at the Door, an Apologia for my life." The Oxford Dictionary defines an apologia as "...a formal written defense of one's opinion or conduct." It is my belief that Sam Shoemaker's apologia describes Howie and his conduct towards alcoholics, addicts, their family and people who love them. See appendix page 131.

Donald R. Hays, D.J., NCACV, CACII
Addiction Case Manager

I met Howie in the early 1970's when he referred alcoholics and drug addicts to me for hospital detox. We soon became close friends as we worked together in caring for alcoholics and other addicts in the hospital and as outpatients, and later in rehab programs. We worked together in the Whole Person Health Center psychiatric day hospital, where Howie directed the evening rehab program as a certified addiction counselor. He later worked for a rehab program as an excellent counselor and interventionist.

I have been blessed by my long friendship with Howie as a gifted colleague providing hope and healing for hurting people.

Darvin W. Smith, M.D., Addictionologist
Past President ISAAC (International Substance Abuse & Addiction Coalition), Diplomat of the American Board of Addiction Medicine

I always look for Howie when I'm at a group meeting. Having Howie in the room means not only that we are in a safe place where conversation can be a healing force, but also that "Howie Hugs" follow. A full-on Howie Hug is an embrace of love and care, an acknowledgement of a person's worth, a reinforcement of one's dignity. I wait in an informal line with others who really need those hugs so that we can absorb some of his compassionate, positive attitude with us into the world beyond the door.

Jeannie P.
Recovery Group Member

Published by Retelling
www.Retelling.net
Produced by Samizdat Creative
www.samizdatcreative.com

*For my brother, who died at 34
because he never got help.*

*And for my wife Pat. Without her intervention I
would not be alive today.*

Contents

Preface—A Compassionate Man   12

Introduction   16

Part One—No Hand on His Shoulder   21

Part Two—Steps to a Compassionate,
Successful Intervention   55

Part Three—Recovery, Finding an
Interventionist, and Costs   99

Part Four—Lessons from People with
Experience in Alcoholics Anonymous   108

Part Five—More Stories from the Front
Lines   115

Part Six—Checklist for a Successful,
Compassionate Intervention   127

Apologia—I Stand at the Door   131

A Compassionate Man

This book is long overdue. Howie has organized and led countless interventions for families and friends of seemingly hopeless alcoholics and drug addicts. His story will guide others in conducting such interventions in an honest and effective manner. I am both honored and pleased to write this short introduction to Howie's experiences and his suggestions on preparing for and conducting interventions—to save the lives of alcoholics and addicts who otherwise probably will die alone.

Howie appeared in my own life in 2001 when I was desperate to quit drinking alcohol and take back my life.

My mind was ready to both admit my addiction and to learn new ways of living without alcohol. In meetings that I attended, the first matter I addressed was to see whether Howie was among us. When he was, I listened and then did my best to implement his advice.

I had learned about Howie's long years of experience in sincerely supporting, and intervening for, thousands of people who wanted to live sober lives. Early on Howie and his beloved friend Whitey personally visited people who were truly "down and out" – drunk or drugged – and hopelessly struggling, living degraded addicted lives. Howie and Whitey went to places others would not go, and therein placed themselves in danger due to their compassion for troubled human beings.

Howie became extraordinarily well known in our community. Word of mouth identified him as one who helped those who were killing themselves slowly or quickly by drinking and/or drugging. He began to organize and lead family and close friend interventions for alcoholics and drug addicts.

It is now 2012, and Howie has become a hero for the more than 2,400 families whose loved ones and friends he has shown the way to leave the lives of addictions and terrible consequences. Howie loves human beings and he gives of himself to help others arise from the horrors of addiction.

Convinced of the help Howie could give many more hurting people, I had an idea. We needed to find a way for Howie's wisdom to be available to families and friends who are geographically dispersed without the possibility of meeting Howie in person. Why not a book that details both his personal experience with addiction, and then his guidelines on interventions for addicts.

Howie agreed to allow me to interview him and record our sessions. We spent many useful hours during which I asked questions and he responded with appropriate expertise and passion. The recordings were transcribed and became many documented pages. Truly humble, Howie balked at having his story displayed in print. Now I am utterly happy finally to introduce this wonderful book that is long overdue and will change the lives of so many otherwise hapless human beings.

My deepest appreciation goes to Mary Beth Lagerborg whose expertise is in writing documentaries like no other person I have had the pleasure to meet. My writing skills are of the boring academic style. This book is not only important, but it is also very readable.

So, please utilize this book about the "Skinny Irishman" as Howie describes himself. And thank you, Howie, for helping me change so that I easily can say that I am living the best part of my life today.

—Dale Meyer , Founder and Chairman,
Western Partners Worldwide

Introduction

At our first meeting at a coffee shop, I watched out the window as Howie climbed from his truck, stretched out his long, lean frame, and slung his portable oxygen tank over his arm as casually as a woman would her purse. He came to our meeting reluctantly, I knew, because he didn't want to call attention to himself. But Howie is now 78 and in poor health, and people who care deeply about Howie persuaded him that it had to be told. On this he did agree: If it would help even one person to tell his story, he was for it.

Howie has no college degree nor medical credentials, yet in the last 46 years he has coordinated more than 2,400 largely successful addiction interventions, and is considered the Godfather of Intervention by nationally-known treatment centers. Many people owe their lives to Howie. Many others would like to understand what he knows, in order to help their own loved ones who are in deep trouble.

Howie has thick white hair and a trimmed but hearty white mustache. His salt and pepper eyebrows bristle upward above his glasses. He is proud to be an American-born Irishman, although a wayward one, as he would say. Quickly I discovered him to be a great story-teller, with frequent waving of hands and punctuations of laughter. Yet his stories are not embellished. They get to the crux of who we are—human beings, all of us, as he says—created by God, and worthy of another chance.

After a couple of sessions at the coffee shop, I met Howie early on a Saturday morning at a recovery group meeting. Howie carries in his pocket a "chip" that commemorates his 46 years of sobriety, and he attends recovery group meetings each week.

I arrived late and looked around a jam-packed room of more than a hundred people sitting on folding chairs. I honed in on Howie sitting in the row along the front wall. His was the first seat to the right of the meeting leader. Relieved that Howie had not saved a seat up front for me, I took a chair along a side wall. The group was similar to what I might see in the doctor's waiting room: a variety of ages (except children), sizes, and by their tattoos and attire, life-styles. A man and a woman worked the room with coffee carafes, refilling and joking.

If it weren't for the white hair and mustache, and the portable oxygen by his knee, I might not have recognized Howie. He was coiled down low in his chair, seemingly incognito, and was quiet and pensive throughout the meeting. As several people shared observations and stories, Howie didn't say a word.

After the meeting I worked my way against the dispersing crowd toward the front where Howie sat. I noticed that a gentle line formed by his chair, people who wanted to talk with him privately, so were willing to wait. A woman sat in the seat next to him and held his hand when it was her turn. Howie made no attempt to rise or to leave until the line was gone.

At our next coffee appointment, I asked Howie about the meeting, and why he sat up front. He said he always does. It was about seeing and hearing. He needed to be where he could see people to hear them well. But he admitted that he likes the spot too: "I sit up there and people come up and give me hugs and give me coffee and ask me where my oxygen is and harass me a little bit and that's a big part of it," he said.

This book contains Howie's years of wisdom and experience on conducting positive, compassionate interventions. It begins with the story of Howie's addiction, and of his commitment to help anyone he can to get the help that they need. Then he explains his intervention method, and the steps necessary for thinking through, planning, and accomplishing one. Additional resources include what Howie has learned about addiction and recovery from 46 years in a recovery group, and things to consider in selecting an interventionist.

Throughout the book, Howie's intervention stories demonstrate some outcomes to anticipate—positive and negative—in order to help you plan a successful intervention.

Although Howie's own addiction and the majority of his interventions have dealt with alcohol, or alcohol and drugs, his wisdom as an interventionist applies across a broad range of addictions. The treatment options would vary, but not the basics of how to train the spouse, sibling, parent, co-worker or friend who may be on the intervention team. No matter the addiction, the point is to take a team of individuals, some of whom may be hurt and angry, and help them to be united, compassionate, and sensitive in the intervention, so that their message can be received.

Howie defines a successful intervention as one that persuades the addict to get help. He wants to help you help them to get the help they need.

Howie's experience will give practical advice and encouragement to anyone who desperately wants to save a loved one who has spiraled downward into addiction. The things Howie would most want to give you are help and hope. He would not want to think he had let you down.

—*Mary Beth Lagerborg*

No Hand on His Shoulder

In my hometown, when I was a boy my family worked a farm on shares and lived in the big farmhouse. And of course, on shares you don't make any money. You do all the work and the owner of the property and livestock gives you half if there's any profit. But you get to live there without paying rent.

I remember I was a month short of seven when my father died of stomach cancer in 1941. He'd be lying in the downstairs bedroom moaning from the pain, because the morphine no longer worked for him. A tremendous odor came out of the room, and Mom wouldn't

[1] Many names have been changed. Masculine pronouns are used when text refers to male or female, merely for simplicity.

let me go in to see him.

My dad was well-respected and liked: a gentle, caring man. Dad did not drink. However, most of the men on my father's side died of alcoholism and the other diseases that are due to alcoholic drinking.

When my father died, my mom had four children. My older sister Elizabeth, who was nine, was physically and mentally disabled. I was seven, my brother Ben was three, and Laura was just four months old. So it was tough for my mom. Of the emotional support that Mom had to give, a high percentage went to Elizabeth because of her needs. She got the most of it, the most attention, the most kindness, and the most time with Mom. Then Laura got the next. Ben got a little bit. And I didn't get any of it. In fact, a lot of my life, until after I got sober, and connected with my wife Pat, I did not have inside me what needs to be inside me to be an effective human being. Just did not learn it.

When I grew up, I wanted to do something that had freedom to it, like be a long distance truck driver. And I did not want to be connected with people who expected me to be the star, because that's what they expected me to be in my family.

I went to Catholic high school, and my mother cooked for the nuns. Mom would be there when the nuns ate lunch, and they would tell her how I behaved in my classes. That was not an ideal situation.

I used to go to church with my aunt and uncle, and I'd see families there with kids, and the kids were holding their mother's hand or their mother put her arm around them, patting them on top of the head and stuff. And as a boy of nine years old I fantasized that was going to happen to me. It never did, but the fantasy helped reduce some of the pain.

As time went on and I grew a little older, different fantasies came. They were effective in my life, until it got to the point where I discovered alcohol would work quicker, and so I would use that. Alcohol became my primary reliever of pain, but the fantasies never completely left. I started drinking at around 14, but I really got into it by the time I was 17, and drank until I was 31.

When I got out of high school, I went to work at a meat packing house in my hometown. Working in a place where there's killing and blood can seriously affect someone like me who wasn't emotionally stable. I used to start the morning at one of the three tough bars near the meating packing house. Then at 9:30 we'd have a break and I'd run out and get a beer and a shot. At lunchtime I'd go back to the bar.

I joined the army as an act of defiance. The girl I went with through high school was going to become a nun. I noticed that she told her fellow classmates, "Now I'm going to work for a few months, and then I'm going into the convent. I've made all the arrangements." As it got close, they held all kinds of parties, and everybody was huggin' her. I thought, *if I tell those people that I'm going into the Army, I'll get all that.* But it didn't work.

That was during the days of the draft, and every young man had a draft number. I went down to the draft board and said, "Push my number up." They did, and I went into the Army at 19, in 1954. I played on an army basketball team, and hung out with two guys who were also alcoholics.

When I got out of the army in 1956, I went back to the meat packing house for 14 months, and then rode to San Francisco with a guy I knew. We stayed at a boarding house and I got work at the Slade Lock Company. But when my friend with the car moved out of the boarding house, I didn't have a way to get to work. I was kicked out of the boarding house because I couldn't pay rent, and that was the beginning of living on the streets.

In the beginning, I was still in pretty good shape. I was drinking heavily, but hadn't lost too much weight. I lost an awful lot of weight over the years I drank. I was put in the hospital—I can't remember why—and while I was there, I called my mom and told her that I got hurt in a forest fire in San Francisco. Later, when I returned home, all the people in the recovery group teased, "This is Howie, the only recovery group member who got hurt in a forest fire in San Francisco."

I went to the recovery group many times in the years that I lived in my hometown, when I got enough pressure from my mom or later my wife. I'd sit in the back of the room with my buddy Patrick and my brother Ben and we'd make fun of people: "Look at that guy. His hair starts up here instead of here like ours does. He's old. I think he drives a new Buick. I bet he just sold all his hogs. If we ever get that old, we'll stop too. We'll be too old to have fun." Patrick and Ben always agreed with me.

Unfortunately, in the recovery group they couldn't find enough young people to sponsor, or mentor, other young people. We were human beings who needed to connect with other human beings our age, and in my case, I connected with unhealthy human beings who were doing the same things I was doing. I wasn't going to hang out with people who said, "Howie, you're crazy. You need to get help." I was a binge drinker, and sometimes I'd go on a binge on my way home from a recovery group meeting.

When I met Pat in 1960, I was still drinking heavily. I met her at a Catholic singles group dance, and I hate to dance. But it was a great dance hall, and I'd been going there for years every Saturday night. It closed at midnight, and then my brother Ben and I'd go to bars in a wild town, across the river, that stayed open until 3:00 a.m. Now I don't know why my new girlfriend Pat stuck with me, but she did. We were married September 4, 1961.

My brother Ben was also a drunk, in some ways worse than I was. He was living with Mom because he kept getting kicked out by his first and second wives. Mom'd call me about 6:00 on Sunday morning, and she'd say, "Would you come over to the house? Your brother's asleep in the front yard, and people are going to walk by to go to Mass. I don't want them to see him." It made me angry, but I usually put on my pants and went over there fast enough.

Once I married Pat, I really tried to straighten out, but I'd been too long in that lifestyle. I had absolutely no coping methods. So I would stay sober for four weeks, sometimes six weeks. Then I'd binge drink, in Minneapolis or Chicago, sometimes Rock Island, Illinois. I'd go and stay in those towns as long as I could stay. I can't remember how many towns or how long. When someone told me the things I'd done the night before, I wouldn't be able to defend myself.

I worked and was fired from several different jobs, but I finally got a hell of a nice job for a local mortgage company. I'd go into little communities and work with the realtors. I had a company car and an expense account. When a family sold a house and they closed on it, when they got the money and everybody was in a good mood, they'd go out for a few drinks. They always invited me, and I would go happily.

After one such celebration, I was coming back crossing a major river when I hit the side of the bridge, broke my jaw, and left the scene. My friend Patrick picked me up and drove me home. About 24 hours later, a cop knocked at my door. My teeth had been knocked down and my jaw was broken. I was a mess. He said, "You were drinking and hit the bridge."

I said "No, no, hell no."

He said, "Yeah, right, you don't look like you've been in an automobile accident. We're charging you with driving under the influence."

My boss called me and said, "You're a hell of a guy, Howie, and we could have made a lot of money together." But he said, "You've gotta go. I hate to do this to you."

When I went on a binge, Pat would lock the doors in the house, pull all the blinds and not answer the phone. She wanted no contact with the outside world, because she feared people would talk about her and judge her for my actions. Her self-worth was sinking rapidly. Cruelly, because I was being a smart-ass, I nicknamed her "The Spook."

Once I'd been gone for three days and snuck in the window in the middle of the night. I don't know what I was thinking—that maybe she hadn't missed me? She was standing there with a hammer and almost hit me, because she thought I was an intruder.

By that time we had three children. My mother used to say to me, "'If you loved Pat and those little kids, those wonderful little kids, you wouldn't drink.'" What she didn't understand is that I could not *not* drink. It had nothing to do with my lack of love for Pat and the children.

Finally Pat had had enough. When I came home from my last junket, as she called it, she said to me, "You look horrible. I'll get you something to eat." I thought I was in the wrong house, because that wasn't the way she usually greeted me. Usually she was mad. She said, "While you were gone, I talked to some people from the recovery group and Joe's wife who has lots of experience with alcoholics. I love you very much. So do the kids. But I'm not going to live this way, and I'm not going to allow the kids to live this way. I've arranged for you to go to treatment. You can either go tonight, or you can go in the morning. But if you don't go, this will be the last night you'll stay in this house. Joe will take you, and Father Beck will go if you want. You make up your mind."

A thought went through my mind—of course I was angry—that I could get along without this skinny Irish wife, but I couldn't get along without the three kids. The most meaningful thing in my life was those children. And so I went, on May 28, 1966. I think I drank on the way.

In those days the only treatment center was the well-known Hazelden in Minnesota, and we didn't have the money for me to go there. So like a lot of people from our region who went for treatment, I went to the state hospital, which was then called the insane asylum.

For 72 hours I was locked up with the criminally insane. They gave me Valium. I went through detox, but I did not have delirium tremens[2]. I stayed there for six weeks, and my older sister Elizabeth was then living at the same state hospital long term.

I remember that while I was in the state hospital, a psychiatrist said to me, "Congratulations, Howie, you have achieved your goal. In grade school you probably made up your mind that you wanted to be in the state hospital as an alcoholic."

---

2 Also called d.t.'s: a violent delirium with tremors that is induced by excessive and prolonged use of alcohol.

* * *

Sobriety

When I went home after six weeks, sober, I was 6'1" and weighed 131 pounds. Joe was at my house about every night picking me up and taking me to recovery group meetings. He was my sponsor or mentor, and like a father to me. He's been gone a long time, but I still have his photograph on the refrigerator.

And I took Antabuse. A lot of people in our recovery group would disagree with me on this, but taking that when I came out of treatment and going to these meetings were very big factors in my being sober today.

Joe used to tell me, "You have to change from drinking thinking to sober thinking." He said, "As long as you stay with people who are relapsing and drinking, you're going to have drinking thinking. You're going to blame other human beings. You're going to say those who are sober are phonies. You're going to say, 'That recovery group ain't for me. Who the hell wants to be like those guys?' Your whole attitude is going to be negative and critical, without acceptance of responsibility for your own life or actions."

I didn't understand this at the time. But after I was sober awhile, it sure as hell made sense. He said, "You've got to change that thinking, because you don't have a lot of stability in your life. Whoever's the strongest in this drinking thinking is going to have great influence on you. So you've got to get over here, where there's sober thinking. And in sober thinking, whoever's on the strongest program, whoever has the strongest personality, is willing to share the most, will suck you in. And then you'll start thinking the way they think. And then you have a pretty good chance for survival."

Many people go to counseling, but if they just stop with that, they don't move forward. Someone needs to take them by the hand. Joe said, "Hell, Howie, you don't know how to do this. Walk with me." And his wife and others did the same thing for Pat.

So I was sober, 31 years old, and I couldn't find a job. For a short time I worked for a construction company, and much of that time we worked on a project at John Deere. They wanted to fill in a big concrete pit, so they could put machines on top of it. We used jackhammers to break up the side walls, so there I'd be trying to hold up a jackhammer. Guys watched, laughing. The first couple of nights I'd come home and my wrists hurt so badly that I couldn't feed myself. So I started applying for jobs again and finally got the best job of my life at a company that made ski boots.

The owner of the company played a very important part in my life. He found a young man deep in the woods and led him out. And kept leading him. He was a rascal, but sometimes rascals do good too.

He knew my reputation before I went to work. But he hired me, and put me in the molding department in the factory as a laborer. It stank and was hot. We put plastic in a mold, and the mold in an oven. But I'd been on the job only two or three months when they put me in charge of all the finished goods and purchasing. The company was growing rapidly.

Recovery Through Giving Back

Meanwhile, Joe kept me busy as blazes. Besides teaching me sober thinking, Joe took me out right away on calls for help with an alcoholic. You go listen to the person and tell your story and see if you can help. You try to give them hope. Joe was throwing me in a car and hauling me everywhere. I've spent a lot of time sitting in cars talking to guys.

In the recovery group Joe had to get speakers for institutions that dealt with alcoholics and drug addicts. Since I was the youngest in the group and already sober, he thought young guys would listen to me better than to someone older.

One time he took me up to the northern part of the state to a pre-release prison camp. After the meeting a young man came up to me with tears in his eyes. He told me why he'd ended up in prison. He said, "I hit a man with my car when I was drunk. I didn't even know I'd hit him. Then I drove home, and parked under the streetlight. My wife looked out the window and came out yellin' and screamin' that a body was on the hood of my car." That is a horrible way to live.

I will never forget one of the early calls that I made with Joe. We went to a house and walked through the kitchen, where five or six kids sat around the table, looking scared. One of the boys pulled on my sleeve, and said, "Mister, will you help my dad?"

I responded, "Yes, I will, son."

His father was hostile to us when we went into the living room to see him. We took great verbal abuse, and after about 20 minutes Joe said, "We need to get the hell out of here." As we passed back through the kitchen, only the one little boy was left. He tugged on my sleeve and asked, "Mister, did you help my dad?" I said that I had tried, but no, I did not help him. The little boy said, "But you told me you would."

Joe and I walked toward the car and I said that this call for help work was bullshit. I didn't want to go any more. It was too difficult, too painful. Joe turned around so he could look me in the eyes. "Howie," he said, "if you refuse to help another human being because it's too painful for you, you might as well go back to drinking now, because you will."

From then on, I never failed to go when I was asked. There was always a chance that who I met would become and stay sober. I learned from Joe that we get well by giving back. Joe said, "Howie, if you want to feel good about yourself, you reach out to another human being. Even if it's a sacrifice, and even if it's a big sacrifice."

Once I got sober, I realized that my own family needed help too. My mother needed me to take her on visits to the state hospital to see Elizabeth. I'd take my mother and my sister Laura. My brother Ben had disowned Elizabeth.

I noticed that every morning Elizabeth parked her wheelchair facing the elevator where people came down for breakfast. As I sat with her observing, eventually I realized that she just wanted someone to acknowledge her. To think of her as a human being. Eventually, some of the people would sit down and eat with her, and you could tell that they were showing a form of acceptance that she could understand. If you sat there and listened, it wasn't a conversation like the rest of us have. But there was an acceptance. I think when that happened in her life, she no longer fought the fact that she was institutionalized.

And of course Elizabeth loved to be loved. She used to ask me, "Do you love me?" And she'd say, "You know I love you." She comprehended this to whatever depth she could understand. And I think she got to the point where she believed that Mother, Laura and I did love her.

* * *

Moving to Colorado

After I'd been with the company for three years, I was transferred to Colorado, in 1969. Olympic skiers were helping us design ski boots, and we had a horrible time getting Olympic skiers to our little hometown. My job was a God-send. I knew I couldn't fail unless I drank. I was Purchasing Agent and Materials Manager. One of the reasons the owner liked me had to do with the tremendous amount of competition among companies trying to make classy ski boots. He knew that suppliers would take us out and try to get us drunk so that we'd tell them all kinds of secrets. He said to me, "I know that you're going to keep your mouth shut. You're going to be sober."

When we moved I immediately joined another recovery group, which at that time was about eight people. And there was no family of alcoholics support group, so Pat started one that met on the same night.

Whitey moved to Colorado the same month and year as I did, and we went to the same recovery group for the first time on the same night. I'd been sober three years, and he'd been sober two. He was older than I was. He wore thick glasses and couldn't see worth a damn, so he couldn't drive most of the time.

Whitey'd been a sheep buyer for packing companies. I asked him one time, "How the hell did you drive to Texas and Missouri and Oklahoma and all over Colorado? You can't see."

"Oh," he said, "I was drunk anyway, so it didn't make any difference."

He was a friend that I really became attached to because of his gentleness and compassion. There were not a lot of people doing calls for help with alcoholics where we lived, because the group was so small. So Whitey and I took it upon ourselves to set up the answering service, take the calls, and go out to help some poor soul. My employer was very generous with my time for this, say if I needed to I could get off at 3:00 in the afternoon. Whitey worked at a hotel and restaurant, and they were good to him too.

We started recovery studies in the early days. Whitey was more spiritual than I was; we were a great team together. Alcoholics would attach to me more than Whitey at first. As a guy said, I was the "logger" and Whitey the "finish carpenter," and you needed them both.

We did some things we shouldn't have done. We'd go to apartments during domestic disputes. Or places where we could have been harmed or killed. We are lucky we did not kill somebody by our being there.

The areas where Whitey affected me the most were spirituality and forgiveness, and he taught me patience. He was an extremely patient man. Being a patient human being became important in my relationships and in the recovery group, but especially later in doing interventions. If you're not patient, you're going to miss some interventions that if you had been patient you could have completed.

Once in the middle of the night we got a call to help a man in a motel, to see if he needed a safe place to detox. The man was lying on the bed in the motel room drunk and covered with blood. He said that while he was sleeping a man jumped through the window and claimed that the woman who had been in bed with him was his wife. The man and his son beat him up and left with the woman. He said he didn't know how the woman got into the room; she must have come in the window. He told us lies about the whole deal. Whitey and I had talked to him in the past, and I had taken him to a hospital only a few weeks before to get a safe detox. This time he wouldn't go to the hospital or to a detox center with us, so we left him in the room. Walking to the car, I told Whitey that I was done with this guy, and that I wouldn't put forth any effort to help this man in the future.

Whitey looked me in the eye and asked me, "Who do you think you are? Do you think you're God?" He reminded me that we were only to carry the message, and the results were in God's hands.

In this case, the cops took the drunk man to the hospital the next morning. He was in the hospital a few days, started to go to a recovery group, and was sober when he died several years later.

Whitey taught me that we had Someone more powerful than us with us, in much the same way that Joe taught me about sober thinking and about service.

One thing you find out early is that it's easier to help somebody who's not a close friend. Those are the ones that'll tear you up most if you can't help them, like my friend Patrick. Growing up together, Patrick was strong, handsome and intelligent, and we often drank all night. My mother said he was a bad influence on me.

Patrick married into a wealthy family and had a nice wife who was a nurse. He continued to drink even though he owned a farm and had four children. After I got sober, I went to Patrick and tried to convince him that he had to stop drinking or risk losing his family and the well-equipped and financed farm. Patrick said he knew that he needed to stop. He went to recovery group meetings with me. I helped him on the farm, and he went to Catholic Church meetings. But suddenly he stopped going to the recovery group and said that he would stay sober on his own. That's dangerous.

Sometime after I moved to Colorado, Patrick bought a bar and hired my brother Ben as a bartender. Both of them drank heavily.

Ben visited me and asked if I would get jobs for Patrick and him at the company where I worked. The two of them thought this relocation would solve their drinking problems. I told Ben that I'd try to get them jobs, but only after they'd been sober for a year. Ben pleaded with me that if they could get out of the bar business, they could stay sober. But I stood by my one-year sobriety decision.

Six months later, Ben was drunk and got into a boat

on a river. He stood up and a dam cable hit him on the head, knocking him out of the boat, and he drowned. It took three days to recover his body. Patrick came up to me at Ben's funeral and said to me, "Ben would be alive today if you'd given him a job in Colorado."

Some time later Patrick's wife called him and said she was filing for a divorce. Patrick lived in an apartment; he was isolated and drank. He wouldn't acknowledge me. One day Patrick placed a hose in his car's exhaust and killed himself.

To this day it has not left me. These were two men whom I tried to help, but I did not do all that I could do, and they ended up dead. I will never know whether a job at the company where I worked would have prevented this tragedy.

I remember back home getting calls from my mom at night saying, "Ben's with Patrick and I think they're out drinking in the cemetery." I'd go out there and try to get them to leave and go home, and they'd give me a bunch of guff and I'd say, "All right. Go ahead. One of these days your names are going to be on some of these stones."

But I think it would have been better, at least for Ben,

and maybe Patrick too, if somebody had helped them not connected to them. I wish someone had.

It's an absolute miracle and God was extremely kind for me to get out of the heavy drinking town of my youth. Because, you see, Patrick didn't get out of there. My brother Ben didn't get out of there. It left me thinking, "You need to reach out to other young people, who are walking the same path. You just need to do it."

My buddy Whitey got cancer, and by the time it was diagnosed, he only lasted six weeks.

So I went over to see Whitey. He lived in a mobile home, and we sat down on a swing on the porch, and the first thing he said was, "I'm going home!" with great exuberance. He said he was gonna see his wife. And I thought, *That's the way I want to go.*

I can't help but grin when I think of this. We were sitting there on the swing, and we both knew he was dying. And I said, "Whitey, when you get up there, I want you to put in a good word for me." And Whitey got this little shit-eating grin on his face, which he had from time to time, and for a few seconds never said a word. And then he looked at me with that grin, and he said, "Howie, I don't think it will do any good."

* * *

From Calls for Help to Interventions

In 1969, when we moved to Colorado, there were tremendous numbers of hippies roaming around. Some of them were wild creatures, the rainbow family, and they were doing a lot of drugs. They camped out in the foothills of the Rocky Mountains and people were afraid to go up there, even the cops. Everybody seemed to be going to San Francisco, and our community was a stop-off. There were crowds waiting to hitchhike, going to the next stop, probably in New Mexico.

There was a judge in town whom I didn't know well, but I wasn't in the recovery group very long before he called me and said, "Would you or some people from your group be willing to come down and talk to some of the prisoners?"

I said, "Yeah, I would," so I went down. I asked some guys in the recovery group to help, and said, "Now there's two things you need to know. Number one, they'll want to ask you for your history. Number two, they're going to take your picture and fingerprint you." And some of them said, "They don't need my picture

44

and my fingerprints. They've already got them."

At that time, Dr. Darvin Smith, who was a medical doctor and an addictionologist, ran a methadone program. He worked with Memorial Hospital to create a locked ward. He would bring people off the street to the ward, and call us at the recovery group, and we would talk with these people at night.

I had a lot of respect for Dr. Smith and what he was doing, and even while I was still working with the ski boot company, in 1976, I went to work part-time for the Whole Personal Health Center, which was a residential treatment center operated by Dr. Smith. He wanted me there when they brought in the drunks, so I worked there nights and on Saturdays.

Dr. Smith would put his patients in detox and then ask me to work with their families, helping them to approach the patient to get treatment. That led to my going along on interventions that some of the larger labor unions or corporations would do for their members or employees who were in danger of losing their jobs. These were largely peer interventions, with co-workers. Perhaps the spouse would be the only family member involved. I'm thankful that I got my feet wet in peer interventions, because they're much less emotionally intense than family interventions. Intervention work was a little different, I learned, than our recovery group taking calls to help with alcoholics. The purpose of the answering those calls is to give hope. But the purpose of intervention is to help somebody to get help.

Eventually I left the ski boot company, and worked part-time for the Whole Person Health Center, and part-time at a nationally respected treatment center. Some board members from the treatment center eventually came to me and said, "You're working nights and you're working part-time. We want somebody full-time in the community. Here's what we'll pay and give you health insurance. Will you come?" I talked to Dr. Smith and decided to go fulltime with the treatment center in 1980. They called what I was doing marketing, but I was actually doing community outreach and family interventions.

I have tremendous respect for them as a treatment center. They put the person's needs first. Although they paid me to do interventions, they never put any pressure on me to bring people there when I went out on a call. For example, once I got a call from a family about a hundred miles away, and went down to see what I could do. The woman was in bad shape, and it would be much closer to take her to a treatment center where my sister Laura was director of nursing, than to the treatment center I worked for farther away. I called the nearby treatment center. "Can you get her in?" I asked.

"Well, we have 50 beds. We have 49 filled and another one coming in today. We can't take her," was the reply.

"Well, can I talk to Laura?"

"Laura," I said, "It has to be today."

"All right," said Laura, "bring her down. I'll put her in the nurse's station until there's a bed open." It was that kind of relationship. The treatment center I worked for didn't care where she was taken as long as she was getting help.

Eventually Pat and I had five kids, and it was terribly hard to work so much. I had very little sleep. Pat had lots of the care of the kids, and she also helped me transport women to treatment, and helped with a recovery support group for family members. On occasion each of my five children went with me to pick up people to take to the treatment center. The kids learned a lot that way.

Eventually I started to train other people to do

interventions, working with professional associations, such as physicians, attorneys, nurses, dentists and pilots to help them set up a system for doing interventions. For example, I helped a group of dentists put together a team to do interventions on fellow dentists who were abusing drugs or alcohol.

In the recovery group literature there's a list of questions that basically ask Did I treat everybody in a kind and loving way today? A long time ago I started praying to God, *Please God, help me treat everybody each day in a kind and loving way.* And that increased the amount of love that I got too. There's no question about that.

In fact, I used to write out those questions in a letter to God every night and answer them. I'd be at our recovery group meeting thinking, *God, this really helps, but I don't get home until 11:00.* Then I'd write out those questions and answers. I was talking about it one time at the recovery group and a woman asked me, "Did you ever think of copying the questions?"

* * *

Tough Tasks and Tender Rewards

Now I have done more than 2,400 family interventions, but unfortunately not for Patrick or Ben, because interventions were not done in those days. We're learning about the value of well-planned interventions, yet we're still far from perfect. As I look back I would have said to Patrick and Ben, "Let me get you some help, and I'll work with my company for them to hire you when you get help." I would have asked the treatment center I represented to take them.

Sometimes when I'm called to an intervention and there are kids involved, and I think the kids are going to suffer more than they've already suffered, or the wife is, I really have a tough time.

I will talk about little children if the addict, whom for an intervention we refer to as the identified person, has any. I'll say, "Maybe if you go to treatment your two little children will have a father." Not having had a dad, I'm very sensitive to that.

Once I had to speak at the funeral of a young man who had taken his life, and in the front row were his two young sons. I leaned over and talked to the boys by name and told them that their father was a great, kind man.

But even though it's hard, that's not justification not to do it. I might say to God on the way in, "You know, you got to be with me. Put the words in my mouth and ideas in my head. But damn, it would be nice if you gave this one to somebody else."

I don't think you can ever stop helping somebody because it's hard. If we have the ability and the mechanism to help another human being, I think we have to do it. I want families to know that there is hope. That this is still their son or daughter or mother or father. They can't find them now, but they're still there. I believe that every human being who is in serious trouble should have a chance to get out of it. And there is hope that they will.

I've never really considered quitting what I do, but sometimes I wish I could get out of the pain. One time I was helping at the Betty Ford Clinic in California, working with professionals in treatment, who happened to hate interventions because they had had negative experiences. I went out to get some air, and I walked on the beautiful grounds, and I had my nametag on. Here came the gardener, an older guy with a hat pulled down. We talked for a few minutes. I said to him, "Do you suppose Betty Ford would hire a wayward Irishman as their gardener here?"

He looked at me and put his hand on my shoulder. "Mr. —," he said, "I would come down here and try it in August before I applied for the job."

Over the years that I worked with Dr. Darvin Smith, and also with my recovery group mentor Joe, I learned that we have God-given abilities that are not just for us, they are for the community that we live in. And Dr. Smith is an extreme example of that. Now he travels the world teaching doctors and therapists and psychologists about addiction.

He was in town a few years ago and invited Pat and me to dinner. He was starting a project in Mongolia, where more than 50% of the people were addicted to alcohol. They were okay until the Russians came in and brought vodka. Before that they drank fermented mare's milk. I said if I'd had to drink that, I probably wouldn't have become an alcoholic. Darvin smiled and said, "You probably would have, Howie."

Darvin wanted Pat and me to come help set up a treatment center in Mongolia. But I told him that I have six metal stints in my heart to keep the blood flowing through, and I'm not a young man any more. I don't think it would be a wise move.

But I've been fortunate, because a lot of people come up to me to say thank you. I'll walk downtown and a man will grab me on the shoulder, or a woman will give me a hug, and they'll say, "Thank you." And I'm thinkin', *What the hell are you thanking me for?* And they'll say, "Don't you remember 17 years ago you did the intervention with me?" And of course I don't. But all those hugs and carryin' on, they're good for an old guy.

In hindsight, I was lucky in the development process to have gone through the intervention that Pat did on me, spend six weeks in treatment, learn from watching my sister parked in front of the elevator in the state hospital day after day, and be taken under Joe's wing in our recovery group. I learned so much from people in recovery programs before I started to develop the intervention process that I have used all these years, as well as trained others to use if they wanted to. I was fortunate that most of my early interventions were peer interventions instead of family interventions, where emotions like fear, guilt, anger, distrust, and resentment can be very hard to keep under control, and if they are not kept down, they can stand in the way of the identified person's agreeing to get help. I had the privilege of moving into this area gradually.

Most of the family members on an intervention team do not understand addiction—that the identified person is trying to find a way to make himself feel better, not deliberately hurt others. Team members are not aware that the addiction is the identified person's single most important relationship at that time—and not by their choice. All human beings, no matter who they are, have needs that must be met or life becomes very painful, and they cannot function the way that they were created to function.

An interventionist must take the time to work with the whole intervention team face to face, to help them understand the addiction and come to grips with their emotions. The interventionist helps the team look at the intention behind the identified person's actions, rather than the actions themselves.

It's important to take this kind of time and careful team preparation. Most intervention teams do not want to take the time to consider what it would be like to be in the identified person's shoes. It's so difficult, and probably it's been difficult for a long time, and they just want to get it done and get out of there. But think of what is possible: to help a loved one to finally get help. To save a human being, to help them get out from behind an obstacle and be all that they can be.

PART TWO

Steps to a Compassionate, Successful Intervention

When To Do an Intervention

When a family contacts me about doing an intervention, they've probably figured it was time to do something at least three to six months earlier. Fear may have kept them postponing it, but then something happens: a DUI, a job loss, or something to trigger that it's time. But the thought has been there quite awhile.

Intervention Story: Just Do It

One time I met a father, mother, and sister, and planned an intervention for their son, an alcoholic and drug addict. The family was bewildered about how to proceed. I conducted two training sessions and an intervention was planned for Saturday, with arrangements made to take the young man to a treatment center.

On the day before the planned intervention, the father called me. He said that his son had found a job as a roofer. He had decided to postpone the intervention to see whether the new job would correct his son's addictions. He was still convinced that the son would be able to be sober on his own.

When he asked what I thought about postponing, I expressed my doubts about the son's ability to get sober on his own, and said that I thought intervention was needed. The father was not convinced. I invited the father to call when he was convinced that the son still needed help. On the following Monday the father called to tell me that the son had died over the weekend of a drug overdose.

I stayed in touch with the father, seeing him now and then at his bagel shop. The two of us would cry about the postponement. The father emphatically volunteered to speak with any family members considering an intervention. His message was Do It and Do It Now!

By the time a family member contacts me to do an intervention, I would say it is time to act quickly.

* * *

A Positive Approach

When I began to do interventions, I thought about what I learned from watching my sister Elizabeth by the elevator—to treat other human beings the way she wanted to be treated. To acknowledge them no matter what, to reveal to them in some way that I accepted them, and to find a way to show them some love. These things opened a door. It seemed important to convey to the identified person acknowledgement, acceptance, and love, so that they could receive an intervention.

Some of this understanding came from my own experience with people accepting me. Some people said to me at the recovery group early on, "Sit your skinny Irish ass down on that couch and stay until the meeting's over, and we'll go have ice cream." They knew I loved ice cream, and that I never had any money. It dawned on me the importance of their acceptance and love. Other people in my life who had tried for a long time to get me to change never accepted me as I was. Never accepted me for Howie.

The old approach that families used to take was to

go without any one's help, or at the most with a minister. And they used a great condemning: "You're no good. Look at what you've done to the kids. Poor Mom is suffering." From my experience, and listening to a lot of guys talk about taking calls for help with alcoholics, it dawned on me that this was a very ineffective way to try to get the message across, so I developed an intervention process. And I decided that I would always spend time preparing the people who approached me to do an intervention.

When I began doing peer interventions, with labor unions or organizations, consequences were a very big factor. In fact, a union would call because of looming consequences: the man was going to lose his job; his wife was ready to kick him out. But it seemed counterproductive to me to walk into a hospital room and lay out a bunch of consequences that would make the man in the bed so angry that he'd turn everybody off, and maybe try to leave the hospital. So I told the labor union members and the wife or family member that we needed to have a way to go in so that the identified person would listen to us. We needed to take the approach of what a good guy he was, and how good his job had been, and that he was a good father, if these things were all true. But that all this was being interfered with by his excessive use of alcohol or drugs. The idea was to get the individual's attention, and get him to listen to us as long as we could.

Of course the cause of the problem also had to be addressed. You could spend time saying he was a nice guy, but it had to come back to the reason we were there. And the reason that individual was in the hospital was excessive use of alcohol or drugs.

While I was doing calls for help with alcoholics and working with Dr. Darvin Smith, I thought a lot about the importance of the message that we gave to the people we were trying to help. When going on calls for help back then, the idea was to convince the person that you were as bad or worse as they were. And look–you were recovering. Although the recovery group message was definitely a message of hope, the downside to it was that if you were telling somebody how terribly bad you were, the receiving individual might think, *Well, I'm not that bad yet. I'm not there.*

For example, why would you begin by saying that you drank for 40 years when you were talking to a 24-year-old? Or why would you tell a businessman who had a serious drinking problem but who was successful in his business and even fairly successful in his family about sleeping under a bridge or in the backseat of a car? If you were talking to someone with high morals, despite the fact that they'd been drinking heavily, why would you talk about your sexual affairs?

I decided I really had to be careful how I approached these conversations, and to share my experience—or maybe not share it, depending upon the situation. And to be honest, I was kind of particular whom I took on calls for help with me. For example, a guy like Whitey was good to take unless I knew we were going to talk to somebody who was extremely anti-spiritual. If the wife of the identified person said to me, "Boy, don't go in talking about God to him," then on the day I was trying to get him to get help, he didn't need to hear a bunch of that and be turned off by it.

But there's a good chance people will stay connected with those who acknowledge and accept them. And hopefully love develops. A compassionate intervention must be based on these things—on acknowledgement, acceptance, and love—rather than on threatened consequences or a great blaming.

* * *

Three Essentials for a Successful Intervention

There are three very important parts to any intervention, and the first is the **intervention team**. These should be the right people, based on their relationship with the identified person, and their first-hand knowledge of his addiction. And the team must be well-trained by the interventionist.

Second, a **receivable message** is offered to the identified person. It's a message of hope. The team must present the intervention solution, which is generally that they go immediately into treatment that has been lined up for them. But it must be in a receivable form, like this: "We believe you are a human being like the rest of us with the same needs, but you've developed a technique of dealing with pain that doesn't allow your needs to be met. But they can be met in the future. Just come...."

You can have the most important message in the world, but if the person you are sending it to cannot hear it or accept it, it's of little or no value. Preparing the team to confront the identified person in a loving way is the most crucial element of team training for the interventionist.

The third important part of any intervention is the **consequences**. These are actions that some or all of the team will take if the identified person does not accept the solution that they are offering in a loving way. Although the team must prepare consequences, hopefully they won't need to present them because the identified person has chosen to go into treatment.

The Intervention Team

Begin with the Right Team—The decision of who's going to be on the intervention team comes from my conversations with the person who contacts me, and then from talking with potential team members. These may be people the person who contacted me recommends, or whom I sense, in talking to him, would be good. If an intervention is going to work, the intervention team is absolutely critical, and choosing it can be tricky.

Some interventionists now use a lot of email correspondence with the team. I do not do that. I want to be sitting with them, looking them in the eye. A woman might say to me, "Oh my, her Aunt Alice just loved her." And I'll say, "Well, give me a description of Aunt Alice." And I'll listen. The woman who's telling me about Aunt Alice may just love her, but the poor lady we're doing the intervention with might despise her. The interventionist has to discern these things.

At least some team members must have first-hand knowledge of the substance abuse, maybe from drinking and drugging with the identified person. Some potential team members may be afraid they'll get too emotional, but in my experience tears and such can be a good thing. If a team member doesn't really want to be on the team, I'll assign them a role toward the end of the intervention, and maybe they won't need to talk.

In a few cases I have had to remove someone from the team, because otherwise the team was not coming together. The intervention won't be successful unless the team is all on the same page. You might think, *Well, this is that guy's wife. She has to be on the team.* But she may be so angry and bitter that you shouldn't have her. On the other hand, a grandchild might be good to include.

If the intervention is on, say, a 24-year-old woman,

and her father's a successful businessman who is domineering and manipulative, if the dad's allowed on the team, the daughter's defense mechanism may come up and the message won't be receivable.

If I have a sense there may have been an abusive relationship between a team member and the identified person, I'll talk to the team member privately. If that's the case, that person must be removed from the team. People who have experienced great childhood or youth stress, perhaps sexual abuse, are some of the worst in being able to handle stress of any kind. And they often turn to drugs or alcohol.

Once in an intervention after I described the treatment option, a sister put her arm around the identified person and said, "Maybe now you can deal with the abuse." Abuse that the family knew nothing about. An interventionist trainee, who should have known better, asked, "What kind of abuse is that?"

"Don't answer that," I said. "It's not their business." This was not the time to bring that up. If you don't know about something like this, and there's already a lot of emotion going on, and it gets laid out, it raises havoc with the intervention.

The vice-president of an automobile manufacturer was on the team of an intervention on his daughter, who was in her late 20's. It was a tough intervention, and he was a tough man to have in it. He told her how much he loved her, and she looked at him and she said, "You son of a bitch. You sit here and tell me how much you love me after all the years you sexually abused me." And none of the family had known about it.

I told him to get the hell out of there. He said, "Where do I go?" I said, "Why don't you go back to Detroit? I don't care where you go, but you're not going to stay in this intervention if I'm going to be the interventionist." And of course he didn't like anybody telling him what to do, but he did leave.

It took me two hours to get everybody settled down, and then I talked to the identified person for a long time. A girlfriend who had worked with her also talked to her. It was a nice fall Sunday afternoon, and we sat outside for quite a while. She was very emotional, but finally she agreed that she would go for treatment.

If I had known about that abuse, I wouldn't have included the father on the team.

Sometimes—it's not happened too often—I would

have to say, "The team you put together, in my opinion, is not the team that needs to talk to the identified person. So you either need to come up with some other team members, or if you want I will talk to him alone, but only if he agrees to talk to me. Anyway, we will not do the intervention at this time."

It can create havoc when the team is wrong.

Adjust Team Attitudes—Usually there's only time for two training meetings with the intervention team. In the first one, I try to read their feelings. Usually they're angry and critical. But if we buy into that, it sets us up for a very difficult situation. They have to come to an attitude that will give a message and a solution that the identified person can receive. They have to want to understand and help the person, not punish them. The majority of the people who have chemical dependency problems have not had their needs met for acknowledgement and acceptance and love.

One reason it's so hard to forgive another human being is because we concentrate on the identified person's actions, not their intentions. Now I don't know if ever in my life I got up in the morning and said, "Well, this is Friday the 13th and I'm going to go and work this person over. I'm going to hurt that person." We do what we do because of the pain inside us; it's not our intention to do it. We make other people suffer because we're not aware of what we do to them. So I talk about this, with the intervention team.

I have to be careful when I'm talking to a family that's going to do an intervention, when I'm trying to find out why their daughter is the way she is. Why is she always drinking and drugging? I'll tell them that usually it's from pain in a person's life. The pain is there, and most of us only know one or two solutions to deal with the pain. The daughter's pain is coming from her needs not being met. I've got to try to phrase this in a way so that the family doesn't think that I'm putting blame on them. I'm not trying to say that these needs were their responsibility, or that they have failed. That would be counterproductive to any kind of an intervention. And that's not a judgment for me to make.

In fact, it's not my job, in an intervention, to go to work with the family about the emotional side of what makes a daughter drink so much. They can get into that when the identified person is in treatment, or it may come out if she goes to a local recovery group, and then has to come and make amends with people she has hurt. It's not my role to be an amateur psychologist on them, but to get the team working together for a productive, positive intervention.

But I do explain to the team that lots of times, alcoholic or non-alcoholic, we go without our needs being met. And I think that's a motivation for self-centeredness.

I sometimes tell this story: What if Jeffrey and I had not eaten for three days, and we're just as hungry as hell, and we were getting desperate. Say we sat on a bench in front of the courthouse, and some poor little old lady came by and sat on the bench across from us. She had a brown bag with French bread sticking out the top. We're just so hungry, we said, "Lady, can you please give us some bread so we can eat, we're just so hungry." And if she looked at Jeffrey and me and said, "Eh, you look pretty healthy to me. Why the hell don't you go get a job and buy your own bread?" I'm not so sure that we wouldn't wrestle that poor old lady to the ground and take her bread away from her. Is it because we wanted to wrestle with an old lady? No, it's because our needs weren't met.

And that's often when self-centeredness comes in.

It's necessary to tell the team that for the alcoholic or addict, the chemical is the most powerful relationship in their life. It takes number one position. I often tell my story. I say that in the years that I was drinking, if you ran into me when I was on my binge in Chicago, and you said, "Howie, what's the most important relationship in your life?" being an Irish Catholic, I might have said God, or my mom, or Pat or my kids. But it wouldn't have made any difference what I said, because you could say, "Save me your line. You're not telling the truth, Howie, because you're sacrificing every one of those relationships to stay in your relationship with alcohol." And when I use myself as an example, it's easier for them to receive.

If I'm meeting with a team, and a team member says, "He can't love me, the way he's running. He doesn't come home to see me at night, to eat dinner with me. He's drunk and I get all upset. He can't love me, and I have a hard time expressing my love to him." I suggest that she say something like this to him: "Dave, I love you, but it's very difficult for me to express my love because of your lifestyle." Therefore you're not saying,

"Dave, you're unlovable." You're saying it's difficult for you to express your love. And it's also difficult for the alcoholic and drug addict to express love to people he has hurt.

The identified person already has lots of people around telling him he's bad. The team shouldn't be in that position. You need to go in and convince him that basically he's a good and talented human being who is developing using an unhealthy technique to ease his pain. He's not bad because he's using that technique. It's that the technique he's developed is bad. His self-worth is already terribly low. Why would you want to drive it down further?

Intervention Story: The High-Achiever

Some years ago I did an intervention on a pretty high government official. I flew to Wyoming, where I was met and driven to the Idaho border.

The identified person was still in Washington, so I had a day and a half there before she arrived. I was shown her office, and I walked around. She was VP of a large corporation, a pilot, and had served in a President's administration.

There were pictures of her with the President and First Lady, and a letter on the wall from the

Secretary of Defense. Listening to her two children and the four employees who were going to be on the intervention team, I realized this was a highly intelligent, success-oriented woman who had accomplished a great deal. I tucked that in the back of my mind and conducted training for the intervention.

During the intervention we weren't able to reach her much at all. Her son, in his early 20's, had a serious drug and alcohol problem himself, and had been in treatment multiple times. Her daughter looked like a flower child and admitted to being a heavy marijuana user. When the daughter talked, I could tell by watching the eyes and facial expression of the mother that she wasn't paying much attention. I'm sure she thought, She's a flower child, what the hell is she going to tell me? When the son talked a bit about how much he loved her, in spite of the fact that he had serious problems, I noticed a tear came down her cheek. Her employees told her how wonderful she was, and how much they liked her and liked working for her. One of them was recovering, and another probably should have been.

Anyway, we had been there quite a while, and we weren't getting anywhere. So I looked at her and I said, "Priscilla, I don't think that I've ever been in the presence of an individual who has accomplished all the things that you have. I saw the letter from the Secretary of Defense and the picture of you and the President and First Lady, and the picture of you as a test pilot, and the awards you've received. I've never, ever seen anybody in this situation as successful as you are." She looked at me, and I knew I had gotten her attention.

"But Priscilla," I said, "In spite of all the things you've accomplished and all the awards you've received, there's one thing that you cannot handle. You know what it is, and I know what it is." And she stared at me.

She said, "You're right. I know what it is, and you know what it is, and what are you going to ask me to do?" And I said, "I want to ask you to go to treatment. I'd like you to go tonight. I'm going to fly out, and I'd like you to fly with me."

She said, "Howie, I won't do that, but I'll go to treatment on Sunday." This was Friday. She asked, "Will you and your wife pick me up at the airport and take me to the treatment center?" And I said, "Yes, we will."

If I had not found a way to be able to deliver that message in the simplest form, without any accusing, she would never have gone.

It helped a great deal that I had spent time in her environment. It's important to try and find out all you can about the identified person. If you look at the positive side of her life and point that out to her, she's much more willing to listen to you. Then lay out the fact that alcohol is a problem and it interferes with lots of areas of her life, without anger or accusation. And basically don't make a judgment. You just say, "This is the way it is, and this is the problem." Highly intelligent people for the most part accept that much easier than they accept, "Look at what you're doing to your kids."

Observe the Intervention Team—Let's say I'm sitting in a room with six people who're going to be on the intervention team. One woman has strong opinions. I watch the other people. I keep my ears open to what she's saying. If somebody reacts strongly to her opinions, and somebody else reacts strongly another way, that's a sign to me: Howie, you've got some work to do. I've got to find a way to bring them all together. And as I said, you can't do that with email, because you've got to see their eyes, you've got to look at their faces.

As the team forms, I observe how they communicate with one another, including watching for touch. I watch to see if this daughter touched that daughter when they were talking about intervention on their mother. Do they touch, or are they separated from one another? You can learn a lot about people by watching them, and it's important to learn as much as I can about a team so that I can be prepared to help them work together.

Build Team Unity—I try to understand these people and their relationships, because the intervention team has to be together. On the interventions that I have been part of, few were troublesome, and well over 90 percent had very positive outcomes. I think that one of the big reasons was spending extra time in person with the team. If at all possible we would have the whole team together at each training.

Sometimes one member shares his experiences and feelings for the identified person, and I notice that other members have completely different experiences and feelings. It is important for me to be aware of any disagreement and to deal with it before the intervention, because if the identified person is aware of any team disagreement, he will probably use it any way he can.

* * *

Consider Religious Beliefs—You've got to be careful when you talk about God, the Creator, a Higher Being. Sometimes on an intervention team no one has a belief in God. Sometimes one or several people have strong and vocal beliefs. You have to listen carefully, to pick up on that and keep it toned down.

It's best to talk to the team individually, and say that I'm not trying to change their beliefs. They're entitled to their beliefs. It's just that their beliefs are best kept to themselves as far as the intervention goes, because it can complicate matters and perhaps turn off the identified person.

I personally have a strong belief that God's involved all the way along. So in the first or the second team training session, I will simply say, "It's none of my business what you believe, but if you believe in Anybody up there, why don't you ask for help? If you don't, that's fine. I'm not saying you should."

Find a Comrade—I try to decide who on the team is going to be my biggest comrade, or ally, at the intervention.

This is someone who understands the seriousness of the addiction, and also knows that the intervention should be to the benefit of the loved one, must be positive. I don't tell the intervention team that I'm looking for a comrade; I just watch and listen. I say to myself, "Ah, it's going to be her." And then I get into the intervention and I get the biggest damn surprise. That's happened to me numerous times. That's one of the things that the interventionist has to be prepared for. You might have three trainings and say, "Man, I've got this down. I know who they are, and I know that this guy right here is my ally. He's going to back up what I say." You get into the intervention, and he might not say a single word. But you discover another one who does.

Encourage Honesty—The intervention team must be honest with themselves, the interventionist, and one another. With the help of the interventionist, they have to discover what's in their heart, what is true. No lying is allowed in the intervention. None whatsoever—with the possible exception of the location of the intervention. More on that later. Lying will only come back to haunt you.

It's likely that the team members have bought into the identified person's dishonesty, and may not be able to see the true reality of the situation. That's one of the big advantages of bringing in an interventionist to train them, who has not been attached to the identified person, and so hasn't been involved in their dishonesty. Since the interventionist hasn't enabled the identified person, he can help lay what is real before the team. See pages 112-113 for a fuller discussion of the important topic of honesty.

Assess Possible Suicide or Retaliation—This has not happened often, but I always ask the team, "Will the identified person retaliate against the intervention team, or will they hurt themselves?" I think it's rare that the team doesn't believe, maybe just a little bit, that the identified person is liable to do something, and we need to lay that open and assess it ahead of time. If they say that they're afraid the identified person will kill herself, I say it's not the right time to do the intervention in this way. But let's say they know someone that the identified person likes, and she lives in Chicago. They might say, "If Sally in Chicago could talk to her, it might work. But we don't like Sally, and she doesn't like us, and we're not going to have anything to do with her."

I'd ask for Sally's phone number, talk to Sally and try to get her to fly in. If she didn't come, I'd ask her to send a letter for me to read to the identified person. Then I'd ask Sally to call her and say, "There's a man I want you to talk to." If the identified person gave permission, I would talk to her her and read her Sally's letter.

I don't worry as much about the identified person's retaliating against the team, unless it is a male who has some tendency toward violence.

The retaliation that I have seen has nearly all been marital. In those cases they ended up in divorce. On rare occasions people split up, and the identified person disappeared. But the whole thing was dysfunctional anyway. It's not that divorce is good, but the fact is that the marriage was not working before the intervention. I've not seen violent retaliation that I can recall, although a couple of times interventions were done and the identified person told everybody to go to hell.

* * *

Assign a Speaking Order—In the second or final training, we get down to the logistics. It's important, for example, to determine who speaks first, but a lot more important who goes last, because they'll have to drop a hammer load if it gets to the place where they have to give consequences.

I prefer that the first person to talk has first-hand knowledge of the person's addiction. People on the team may say, "He's probably a bigger drunk than the guy we're doing the intervention on." But I want to have him go up front, because he could say, "What the hell are you thinking about, saying you don't have a drinking problem? You and I get drunk together." It eliminates a lot of the denial, and can open the door.

Then the next two or three people to speak have to be people who can deal with the addiction, but make a transition. They can say, "You know, Gary, it's true. You have this real serious drinking problem that I don't understand, and my heart aches whenever I think about you drinking." So it eases the tension. You do your best to plan how this will go, but of course sometimes you have surprises.

Intervention Story: Speaking Order Surprises

A few years ago I met with an team Saturday morning and afternoon. The intervention was on a person who was well-known and respected in town. We decided to do it at the large, beautiful home of the identified person's girlfriend.

As always, I had the team walk in first, then I came in last and said, "I'm Howie. We need to talk about something going on in your life."

The identified person hugged the other people and just looked at me. He said, "Now I know these people love me. But you dirty rotten effer, I do not know you, so you keep your g.d. mouth shut." And I was supposed to be in charge! I did keep my mouth shut for a long time. It was very fortunate that there were two physicians on the team, whom the identified person respected, and both of them had visited treatment centers. For a long time I just sat on a high stool and drank coffee and ate donuts. So sometimes things happen just the opposite of what you'd expect.

Another time an identified person said to me, "I know this is one of those interventions." I put my hand on his shoulder and said, "You're exactly right. I'd appreciate it if you'd listen to what your family and friends have to say, and then we'll listen to what you have to say."

He said, "All right. They can read their damn

letters until hell freezes over, but the only one I'm interested in listening to is you, because you're a recovering alcoholic." They read their letters and he wasn't even paying any attention to them. He sat on the couch next to me and said, "Tell me a little bit about recovery. Tell me how you stay sober." You never know what will happen in an intervention. You have to be prepared, roll with it, and be persistent.

Choose a Location—In deciding the location for the intervention, the first thing to consider is safety: someplace where there are no weapons, and there's a good chance you're not going to get kicked out of the house. A home is best if you can find one, but preferably not the identified person's home.

It can get touchy, because the identified person might get suspicious if you ask him to go with you to someone's home. This is the one time where I said you might need to tell a lie—about where you're going and what's happening there. It's not the best, of course, but you might need to do it. The identified person might say, "Hell, I'm not going. I'll have coffee with you here or somewhere, but I am not going to that house." In those situations you really have no choice but to do it in the identified person's house. I've done a lot of them that way, but I really dislike it.

Intervention Story: Follow Your Intuition

You need to listen to your gut about the location. One time a friend asked me to do an intervention. We had three intervention team meetings and were set to do the intervention on a young man who was destroying his life and hurting many family members because of his addiction to chemicals. I was not very happy about the idea of doing it at the house where he lived, but the team didn't think they could get him anywhere else without his finding out what was happening.

At the house, there were holes in the walls. I asked the identified person's roommate how the holes got there, and he said that the identified person hit the walls at times when he was high and got mad.

I tried to stop the intervention at this point, but before I could get the team out of the living room, the identified person came out of his bedroom and asked what was going on. He was high and had a wild look in his eyes, even though the roommate had said he would make sure he would not be high or drunk when we came to the house. I think that the roomy had called the mother and told her, but she knew that if she told me I would've called off the intervention, and she didn't want that. So we walked into a dangerous situation.

The intervention started and the mother did not follow the speaking order or say what she had written in her letter, as she had agreed to do in the trainings. In fact, she moved immediately to consequences. She pulled a set of car keys out of her purse and held them up and said that they were the keys to her car that her son had been using. She let him drive her car, and she also owned the house he lived in. She said if he didn't go to treatment, she would come over the next day and set his stuff by the curb for the Salvation Army.

The son came out of this chair to grab her, threatening to kill her, and two of the team members who were big strong men grabbed him and hollered for all the other members to get out.

Somehow the son got away from them and ran out of the house. His mother was just backing out the car, and the driver's side window was open. The son got his hands inside the car and started to choke his mother. I hollered for her to back up, which she did and got away.

I got a call about 3:30 a.m. the next day, and with the help of his roommate and my friend, we took him to treatment.

I learned from this to listen to my own feelings and better

judgment, and not do an intervention just because a friend asked me, which was the case here, and not at a location I sensed wasn't right. Safety must always come first. And, of course, the team needs to be together and do their agreed part. This mother didn't read her letter, or respect the speaking order, but she went straight to the consequences.

Intervention Story: Hospital as an Intervention Location

A hospital is also a good location for an intervention—not in detox, but if the identified person is a patient for some other reason. But of course you must clear it with the hospital staff. One time I did one in a city hospital. The young man had broken off a syringe in his ankle. It was infected, and he was in a lot of pain. I told the family that if they wanted to do the intervention at the hospital, they should clear it with the staff, and then I would come.

The hospital was very cooperative. They moved out the man in the next bed. I don't know what they used for an excuse. Frankly, I don't know if this hospital would ever do it again, because it was a tough one, with yelling and screaming and swearing.

The identified person was 22, and the intervention team was his relatives and an ex-drug dealer who flew from Dallas to be part of the intervention.

We were required to have a hospital employee with us, so they sent in a family representative. This poor older woman stood by me, and I could tell she was uptight, especially when the young man started ranting and raving.

We got to the consequences, and the dad said, "We're supporting you, son. We're helping pay your rent. We're giving you money, because you're not working."

"He's dealing drugs," said the ex-drug dealer.

"And it's over," the father said, "because we'll turn you in to the authorities." The ex-drug dealer would not take him to Dallas. The family would have nothing to do with him. So he had his choice. Either he could go to the treatment center or stay until the hospital released him and go back on the streets. And I think the pain in the ankle was so bad that he knew he needed to get help. Pain is a great motivator.

At one point I asked all of them to leave the room except the mother. And when they opened the door to leave, a bunch of hospital employees were standing outside the door listening, because they had never seen or heard anything like this.

The young man began blaming his mother, but I said, "You're in that bed for a reason, and it's because you broke a needle off in your damn ankle because you were shooting drugs there. You know that. They know that. Get off your mother's back."

"Your mother told me she has terminal cancer. She's not going to live much longer, and the best possible thing you can do for her is to go get treatment and do it today." He started calling me names, and I said, "Hey, that's what I'm here for. But at least give a little concern to your mother, and try to fulfill maybe her last wish."

He said, "All right," and threw in some other words. "Who's going to take me?"

I told him his dad and the ex-drug dealer were, and he did choose to go to treatment.

Be Persistent—Too often an intervention team looks at the intervention as a failure if they do not accomplish the goal and the identified person doesn't get help right then. But a fair number of times if you do an intervention on Saturday, the following Thursday the identified person will call and say, "You know, I've changed my mind. I'm going to go. Is it still available?"

Intervention Story: Leaving the Letters

A mother called me who had talked to a treatment center about her daughter. The daughter had a very serious drugging and drinking problem, and she was in a violent relationship with a man she said she wanted to marry. The daughter had tried to kill him, and the woman who contacted me was sure that it would only be a matter of time before she got the job done.

The treatment center intake person told the mother to be very careful who she got to be the interventionist, because of the danger of the situation.

When I met with the woman, she was upset and fearful, with very little hope of being able to get help for her daughter. We talked for a long time and went to the treatment center to ask the intake person if they would be willing to admit the daughter if we did the intervention and she agreed to come.

After a long meeting the center agreed to work with us, but said that they would need a lot of information about the identified person from me and the intervention team. After discussing with the team the violence and self-harm issues, we had three trainings, all in person, which was particularly important in this situation. On the day that the intervention was to be done, the identified person could not be found. An important member of the team lived in another state and had to return home that night, so we didn't get to do the intervention as planned. The team was very upset and had given up hope of getting any help for her.

They had all written letters that they were going

to read at the intervention. I had them make copies of the letters so that I could take them to the house where the identified person lived and leave them for her. They thought that was a crazy idea, and that she would destroy them and maybe not even read them. However, I convinced them that many times people who have addictions run out of their chemicals in the wee hours of the night, and in an act of desperation may find letters like this, read them, and be willing to get help. This woman did, and 30 days after the day that we planned on doing the intervention she entered the treatment that was going to be offered to her.

Two years later, the mother wrote to me, "All the times that you met with us, the guidance, council, and most of all the hope that you installed in us uplifted us, and she is sober and clean today." The reason I bring this up is to show that even if all others are discouraged, the interventionist must stay with the belief that help may still be possible. It is much easier to walk away from a difficult, fearful situation than to stay and deal with it. But finding a way to deal with it might save a life.

The Receivable Message

The team's message must be receivable, and that means that it must be based in acknowledgement, acceptance, and love for the identified person. I've talked to many people who were identified persons in an intervention and who said "No thanks!" to the offered solution. Even with a good professional interventionist and good solutions, the team may not get the desired result if their message isn't receivable. It's helpful for the interventionist to ask the team during their training how they think they would like the message delivered to them if they were the identified person.

All the team training, and all the emphasis on a positive team attitude, is so that the team can convey a message that the identified person will open their heart to. Something they'll hear and accept. The team is requesting that they enter treatment. How they present the message of what they want them to do, without scolding or blaming, is crucially important.

Intervention Story: What Are Your Dreams?

Years ago a doctor asked me to go see a young man who was a patient in a community hospital. He had a serious alcohol and drug problem, and his parents were at loose ends. He had dropped out of college, was about 20 years old, and had been involved with alcohol seriously for two years.

The doctor asked me to first talk with the family and then go to the hospital to see the young man. The mother and father had given up hope. The sister believed that her brother's attitude was that his drinking was not his fault. He blamed situations and others, and he took no responsibility for his life and actions. Furthermore, she said that he believed that AA was fanatical, cultish, and useless. The sister warned me not to talk with her brother about AA.

So I went into the brother's hospital room and introduced myself. It happened that the brother knew some of my children.

Immediately he said, "I won't have AA driven down my throat." I took another approach and asked, "If you did not have this problem and were not in this hospital, what would you be doing? I would guess that you don't like being stuck in your present state. Probably you have uncles or friends or acquaintances who are doing something that you consider to be worthwhile, and you would like to do something worthwhile. What would stop you from pursuing your goal if you weren't so dependent on drinking?"

He said, "I've sometimes thought that I'd like being a teacher and a coach."

I told him how my dependence on alcohol earlier in my life kept me from doing worthwhile things. I told him that a man believed that I had character and talent, even though I had smashed a car belonging to his company and had been fired for it. The man had confidence in me, but I had to get the alcohol under control.

Then I told the young man that he had a boulder to get around, and that it was okay to ask others to help him get out from behind that big boulder. "Find other people who have gotten out from around the boulder. Stay on the other side of it."

He said. "You're not telling me to go to church or to AA?"

"No," I said, "just talk with people about how to get around that obstacle. Think about it, and I'll come back in a couple of days."

When I came back, the brother thanked me for talking to him and telling him my story. I suggested that he might find it helpful to see Dr. Darvin Smith. "I think that you are seeking people who know how to move boulders," I said. I thanked him and gave him my phone number.

Two days later he called and said he would like to work with Dr. Smith. And after working with Darvin, he decided to attend a recovery group. He earned his college degree in teaching and was a teacher for many years. Now and again we run into each other, and he still thanks me for telling him my story. He says that if I had tried to recruit him into AA, he would not have listened.

I learned from this experience not to stress the horrible things that will happen if the alcoholic lifestyle is continued. It is fundamental and essential to convince the intervention team that we are not going to put the person down. In my own case, my wife Pat simply and determinedly said, "I won't live this way and our children aren't going to live this way, so you go to the hospital and quit harming your family and friends. You are a good person and that is the person we love. If you refuse to get help, then you will have to go your own way by yourself."

In intervention, there must be an honest message of hope, not destruction. It doesn't work to try to scare people into quitting drinking or drugging. The addict's common defense to stories about what happened to others is, "That won't happen to me. I am not as bad as they were. That's not me." Instead, we can ask, "What do you still dream about? Want to be? Is alcohol getting in the way?"

Letter Writing—Interventionists typically ask each team member to write a letter to the identified person, and the letter serves several purposes. I use letter writing to get into the heads of the people who could be on the team and see what they're thinking. Writing helps team members clarify what they think and feel for themselves. And of course the letters communicate that team members care for the identified person so much that they are willing to intervene. I ask everybody to include three things in their letters. First, I want them to talk about how much they care about the person. What are their good qualities? Write about times they've had fun together.

The second part is to write about the seriousness of the problem. For example, "You know, Mom, you're in terrible physical condition, and it's a direct result of drinking and drugging. If something happens to you—and because of your drinking and drugging it could very well be—there's going to be a hole in my heart that no other human being can fill." Often team members will break down when they read the letter to the identified person, but I always felt that, man or woman, tears were not going to interfere with anything. In fact, they're probably a big help.

Then the third part of the letter is the consequences:

"If you do not go, Mom, this is what I'm going to do." In the actual intervention, the consequences from each team member are written in a separate letter that I hold, so that they're not pulled out unless they're needed.

From the letters I try to learn as much about the identified person as I can, and what to talk about. I have to have compassion not only for the identified person, but also for the team.

Finding a Treatment Facility—Many people rely on the interventionist to recommend a good treatment option. This may be a residential treatment center, outpatient treatment, or a good therapist. There are also camps and programs for children who live with addicted parents, which aim at prevention. Much preliminary research can be done online by searching for addiction treatment facilities.

When researching treatment options, here are some of the first questions you should ask of a potential facility.

Interview Questions for Treatment Facilities

1. How long, on average, has your staff been here?

2. How many of your staff members are recovering? It used to be that nearly 100 percent of a staff were recovering, and that's a big asset.

3. What emphasis do you put on after care?

4. Do you have a family program? If so, how many family members can attend?

5. Do you work with sobriety houses?

6. How do you feel about/ what advice do you give about recovery groups such as Alcoholics Anonymous?

Consequences

Once each team member has thought of what they would present as a consequence, I ask them to separate this off from the letter they're going to read to the identified person, and be prepared at the intervention to give this part to me. I don't bring out the consequences unless it's necessary, because it could turn off the identified person and get them angry. But if it becomes necessary,

I might say something like this: "Your lifestyle carries a terrible consequence, and possibly death. There are people in here who care about you who understand that, and you need to understand that. So you need to go get the help that they've planned."

And the identified person might say, "You know, Howie, you're a crazy old goat. Go out and get in your car and get the hell out of here." Then I will say, "Each one of these people has written not only the letters that they read to you, but now they're going to hand to me, and I'm going to give you, their letters explaining consequences that they will have to carry out."

I can't create consequences; the team has to. They're the ones who must live with them. Consequences are usually things like this: "You know we love you, but if you're not willing to get help, you must move out of our house, because you're a bad influence on your younger sister." Or perhaps a member of the intervention team who has been providing financial support for the identified person will say that support is over if they don't get the help that is offered.

In some ways it's softer for the interventionist to read the consequences. The general belief is that interventionists shouldn't display softness, but in my experience softness plays an important role. Most team members don't want to make it easier, softer—they want to get even. If it reaches a point in the intervention where the identified person has refused to get help, the success of the intervention can be in danger because team members may be so angry or hurt. The interventionist may be the only one in the room at that time who has compassion for both the identified person and the team members, because he or she has not suffered because of the addiction. So it's important for the interventionist to take the role of reading the consequences, to soften the emotion.

I learned a good lesson in my own family. Our oldest son was in junior high school, and he came home later than he was supposed to one night. He and I went down to the family room, and I must have put out a punishment like, "You're grounded for three weeks."

"Dad, can I ask you a question?" he said.

"Yes, you can ask me a question."

Irritated, he said, "Why doesn't the punishment ever fit the crime in this house?" I've thought about that over and over. Team members must think of consequences that fit the situation and their relationship with the identified person.

A therapist once told me that intervention doesn't work, because a client of hers who had an intervention done is not sober. But I told her that intervention has only one purpose, and that is to get the individual to go get help. It has nothing to do with what happens after the individual goes to the treatment center or to a recovery group or wherever they go. People get that mixed up, and it often stands in the way of doing an intervention. After an intervention the team needs to ask: Has the goal been attained? Has the identified person gotten help? And if that goal's been attained, what happens afterward, in treatment, is separate from the intervention.

PART THREE

Recovery, Finding an Interventionist, and Costs

Debriefing the Intervention Team

If they're willing, I like to debrief the intervention team sometime after the intervention is over. If the identified person goes into treatment, I talk to the team about the possibilities of the individual getting and remaining sober and clean. One of the critical factors is a safe detox. Another is continuing family support.

The identified person will likely come out of treatment angry because of the intervention. It will take lots of compassion and understanding, but if he jumps on them for being involved, the team should respond with

"We did that out of love for you."

What if the identified person becomes sober and then relapses, leaving the team hurt and disappointed? This doesn't mean he won't be sober again. We have to say, "Come be with us. We'll walk with you. Today's a new day." The more the family does that, the more the chance that the identified person will eventually stay sober. It's a narrow and dangerous path they're treading. It's important not to give up hope.

At the Treatment Center

Family and team members often ask me how the identified person is doing in treatment. The law will not allow any professional to release information to the family or other team members without written permission from the identified person.

But they can contact the treatment center. The interventionist will have given the counselor or intake employee information about the intervention, including the letters. The interventionist is contracted to do the intervention, and once that is completed, his or her role is over.

A treatment center will approve treatment for a certain number of days. I've been told it's 28 days because that's what insurance companies will pay for. But honestly, recovery rates show that if there's some way that a person can be connected with a treatment center for 90 days, the recovery rate goes way up. They don't have to necessarily live in that facility for 90 days, because that gets terribly expensive.

Living Connected

Upon leaving a treatment center, the identified person needs a place of connection in order to live sober out in the world. I would say even the top treatment centers are actually discovery centers. Recovery comes after people get out of a discovery center. Recovery comes when they go to recovery programs, where they connect with people with sober thinking, and people care about them. Somebody who understands needs to turn around and reach down and grab them by the hand and start helping them up, or they're never going to get out and live sober. As the "Big Book" of Alcoholics Anonymous says, "We alcoholics found that we must work together and hang together, else most of us will finally die alone."

Some treatment centers invite recovering alcoholics in the area to come in for a meeting, so that the person in treatment knows some faces and has some phone numbers when he gets out. But if he just says, "Well, I've completed my 28 days, I guess I'm cured," his chances aren't good. Connection is extremely important in our lives. That's one reason why I think that finding a treatment center close to home can be helpful, for the recovery network.

One good option for after treatment is a sobriety house. There are several around the country. Everybody who lives there is sober and clean, and they put men and women in different facilities. In most places it's required that they stay at least 90 days. If you send a person to an approximately 30-day treatment, and then he goes into a sobriety house for 90 days, now he's up to four months, 120 days. You're starting to open the door to give him a half-way decent chance. It's the continuity. You have to get him with people who have sober thinking, away from friends with drinking thinking. I can't tell you how important that is. The ideal would be for him to live in a sobriety house for a year. You can research sobriety houses online by part of the country. They're now classified by the intensity of the program.

When the identified person comes out of treatment, the family should treat him with compassion. Even if he's angry, the team did what they did out of love, and he must know that. Let's say he comes out sober but relapses. That doesn't mean he won't be sober again. They must be kind to him, invite him to be with them. "Come be with us and we'll walk with you." It could happen again and again and again. But sober days do count as days lived without using.

There's no cure for alcoholism. They have to have people who will take them by the hand and walk with them. And the family needs people to take their hands too. I strongly suggest to the intervention team that they go to a family-centered recovery support group.

Finding an Interventionist

Most interventionists work by themselves; it's rare that one is employed by a treatment center. There was a time, and maybe it's still true, that I was the only interventionist employed by a residential treatment center. And I was a trouble-maker.

Treatment centers will recommend interventionists. And you can search for one online. A good place to start is the Association of Intervention Specialists (http://associationofinterventionspecialists.org/).

A good interventionist is a person with compassion and sensitivity. These are qualities that the intervention team is going to have a difficult time identifying inside themselves. If an identified person senses compassion and sensitivity in the interventionist, there's a better chance he's going to listen. There is benefit for all involved if the interventionist has walked the walk of the identified person, is recovering himself or herself.

Inner confidence is another important trait, so that the interventionist has good intuition and can make and stick to hard decisions, like removing someone from the team or changing the intervention location. They need to be able to think on their feet: to assess a situation quickly and act.

The Cost of an Intervention

The cost of the intervention and the cost of treatment must be dealt with before the intervention is begun, so that it doesn't cloud the intervention. In the interventions I do, it's nearly always handled with whomever contacted me for the intervention, and might look like this. I'll say, "How about if we sit down for coffee and discuss the whole thing." I tell her that before the intervention is done she needs to decide—herself or with the intervention team—what method of help will be presented: residential treatment, out-patient, or a very good therapist. She needs to discover the charges, and we'll discuss what I charge.

I explain that I will call the treatment center or treatment option to make sure that all necessary arrangements are made before the intervention, including financial arrangements and what the identified person is allowed to bring with them. You don't want to arrive with the identified person and have someone say, "I don't think he should be here. He should go somewhere else."

I also ask the intervention team whether anyone will

be willing to take him to treatment. We need to have this detail settled first, so he can know how he's going to get there. If the identified person is a woman, I won't take her by myself.

I've heard of people who have had interventions done on them, and the first thing that happened to them when they got to the intervention, or when they got to the treatment center, was that they were asked how they would handle payment. That should all be handled before the intervention. The identified person is nervous and upset and fearful. Why on God's green earth would you throw something like that at them?

Try to find an interventionist who's not too expensive. It upsets me that there are families with little money, sometimes because of the addiction, and they can't get help. There are lots more people who don't have lots of money than those who do, and they're created by the same God, equally as valuable as the rest of us.

Payment may involve people on the intervention team and the identified person, and maybe there will be some help from the chosen treatment facility. Occasionally the treatment center will wrap the bill for intervention with the cost of the treatment, and so insurance will cover it. A few interventionists will charge on a sliding scale. You can at least inquire about these possibilities.

It you can't afford an intervention and residential treatment, at least line up your identified person with a therapist who doesn't charge much, or who will do a freebie here or there, to get them going. Start the identified person moving toward where they need to go. I do not advise families to do interventions without an interventionist, without knowing what they are doing; it's too dangerous.

PART FOUR

Lessons from People with Experience in Alcoholics Anonymous

Lessons about Sobriety from AA

It's impossible to over-emphasize the importance of connecting with a community of sober-thinking human beings in order to achieve and maintain sobriety. Obviously the AA processes are well known worldwide. There are other communities, other ways, but these are some vital lessons from the AA community that are important as preparation for being involved in an intervention.

People come to Alcoholics Anonymous for different reasons. A desire to stop drinking is different than the desire to stop the pain that the drinking has caused, or that a lifestyle has caused. Lots of people come to AA who are tired of going to jail, tired of getting fired, tired of their boss or their wife chewing their tails out. They want to get rid of all that. And they don't reason it through far enough to realize that if they stopped drinking, a lot of that would stop. How insane it is that every single time they need a solution, to get rid of pain, they go to a chemical. It didn't work 300 other times. Why the hell would it work the 301st time? But they still use it.

Still, most of them want to get rid of the pain that they're experiencing. And that does seem sufficient sometimes to keep them at AA until they get to the point of saying, "Yeah, I do need to stop drinking, and I want to stop drinking." But they don't necessarily come in with that attitude.

From evidence about AA, those who benefit from this process often assert that their biggest success factor is staying with the program and moving on with it. It's the people they bond with when they first come to AA that counts. If they somehow connect quickly with people who are very active in the program, and if they find a sponsor, or mentor, who's been in AA awhile to teach and encourage them—if they hang with those people, there's a very good chance that they'll stay with the program. That community with sober thinking is tremendously important. And the identified person will reach out to others, just as people reached out to him.

It's important that their AA sponsor is somebody with whom they can identify. There's now a large, diverse population of people in AA. The identified person is likely to find somebody they identify with, whom they like and listen to.

People don't push belief in God down your throat in AA, God in a certain tradition or way. But in AA there is the acknowledgement of God, the Creator, a Higher Power—whatever you choose to call it.

One thing that AA does well is to celebrate success. You get an annual sobriety birthday chip, and once a month you get a chip for each month you've been sober. It's something to say, "I've achieved" that you can carry with you, in your pocket. You come up when you get it and you get a hug and people applaud. It says that you've done something important and that everybody knows it, and everybody's been through it.

Thinking on long-term permanent sobriety can be

destructive. Say a woman's been sober for a period of time, and she relapses for two days. The 58 days she was sober some people say don't count. But they do count. She lived them. She walked on the face of the earth. She did not drink those 58 days. And two days she messed up.

Or what if a man is sober for 60 days, relapses for three, is sober for four months, relapses for another three days, is sober for six months, and then relapses for another short period. After that relapse he stays sober for months or maybe a year and a half and then has another short relapse. destructive thinking discounts any of that success. Often the prior AA experience is counted as a failure. But it isn't a failure; in my opinion it's not.

People who are recovering need to guard against that thinking too. They may have been asked to serve as a sponsor. If they're working with someone and they're relapsing, and the relapses are farther and farther apart, there's a good chance that they're going to have continued sobriety. But if the relapses are closer and closer together, the chances are not good.

There's lots of humor in AA meetings. People laugh at things the general public wouldn't laugh at, because they have so much in common with people who are hiding something and know all the tricks that they play.

An example of the deceptions alcoholics use is an attorney I know who used to hide his booze in a garden hose. He cut the hose to a certain length and plugged both ends, but the one end had a cap. He'd pour booze in there and hide the hose in the garage. I can't imagine what that must have tasted like, or what it did to the garden hose, but it shows the obsession, and also deception. As addicts we deceive ourselves as well as others, whereas we need the kind of honesty that will eventually let us accept ourselves.

One time I met Smitty, son of Dr. Bob who was one of the founders of AA, and I asked him what his dad thought was most important in recovery. He told me he remembers hearing Dr. Bob and Bill[3] talk about three levels of honesty. The first one is cash register honesty, where you quit stealing if you were stealing. The next level is resume honesty, where you only tell certain things, trying to make yourself look good. But the kind of honesty that makes it possible for you to live with yourself in peace is gut-level or rigorous honesty. Dr.

3 Founders of Alcoholics Anonymous

Bob said that gut level honesty will give you freedom and the ability to accept yourself, so that you can have serenity.

This kind of real honesty is referred to on the chip where it says, "To thine own self be true." Lies stand in the way of our relationship with others, because we can't be our real selves when we're lying. And I think lying also stands in the way of our relationship with God.

One of the challenges I noticed about gut level honesty, though, is that I got to the point where I couldn't tell when I was lying and when I wasn't. When you remove the chemical, alcohol or drugs, that doesn't necessarily mean your honesty changes. Most of us left to our own devices are not going to find reality and confront it. I damn near have to have somebody else involved in my identification of honesty. I deceived myself for so long, even with some self-deception in recovery, in the early stages, that it became hard to get a true look at the reality of where I was with honesty. Sometimes I'm still not able to identify it myself, except with the help of a trusted friend. One of the best ways to do that is through a sponsor.

Sometimes those who come into Alcoholics

Anonymous, at least in the beginning, don't examine their fantasies. If they're going to be who they really need to be, somewhere along they've got to look at reality.

I was talking about reality one day in my recovery group, and a guy raised his hand after I was finished talking, and he said, "Yes, Howie, it is true that those of us who don't want to deal with reality damn near go to any length about it in fantasy and drugs and alcohol. But you know, you can deny reality, you can lie about it, you can push it aside, you can push it down, but someway someday it's going to come up and bite you in the ass unless it's dealt with. And I think the way it bites many of us is we don't get inner peace."

PART FIVE

More Stories from the Front Lines

Intervention Story: The Drug Dealer's Wife

One intervention experience gives a pretty good example of the entire process. I got a call from an 82-year-old woman who wanted to get help for her 55-year-old daughter who had a serious alcohol problem.

As I talked to her about the intervention process, the intervention team, the need for a receivable message, and the consequences, I became aware of two conditions that would make this intervention more challenging than normal. The daughter was married to a convicted murderer and drug dealer who took her car keys and gave her only anything she wanted to drink. The team thought he was trying to kill her, hoping to get her house and her money. And the team said the only place to do the intervention was in her home, and there were guns there.

I asked the mother to have some other family member call me. The next day I got a call from one of the identified person's daughters, and she and the 82-year-old grandmother became my contact people for the intervention planning. I told them the kind of people who would be good for a team, and two days later I had eight family members willing to meet with me. We set up a time and place to meet two nights later. Seven of the eight people came to the first meeting, which lasted three hours.

The first thing I asked each person was whether they feared retaliation from the husband. Did they feel that they or their family members were in danger if they were members of the intervention team? Some of them were fearful, and I was about to call off the intervention when a son-in-law told me that the husband was on a drug run to the southeastern U.S., and would not return for another four or five days. The whole family agreed the life of the identified person was in grave danger because of her physical and mental condition, and that this was their only chance to help her.

I also asked if they thought that the identified person would hurt herself, or any of them, if the intervention didn't result in her going to treatment. They each said that they felt sure she would not hurt any of them, and that they must go ahead with the intervention or the identified person would be dead in a short time, as her doctor had said.

I told them to write in letters what they were going to tell the identified person at the intervention, and I gave suggestions on what I would write if she was a loved one of mine. I told them about what solutions were available, and that they must decide which one or two they wanted to offer her. One of them must make arrangements with the treatment center. I suggested that they give this matter serious thought and prayer, and that we would meet again in two days. I thought that one of the identified person's daughters would be my ally.

At the second team meeting, which lasted about 2-1/2 hours, we agreed to do the intervention at the home of the identified person, and at what time we would meet to go to the home together. The registered nurse who had been helping in the home would make sure that the guns were removed. We set the speaking order.

The team said that denial would not be a problem, because she had been to the hospital many times to detox. I told them that all effort needed to come from a place of love, care, and concern, with no moral judgment, no shaming or attacking her. I suggested that they be aware of the fact that her behavior and actions toward them were not because of a lack of love for them, but because the addicted individual always places the relationship with substance before any other relationships.

The team agreed on a solution to offer, and they made all arrangements for treatment. They decided who would go outside with her and bring her back in if she walked out of the intervention, and who would take her to treatment. They each read their letters to me, and we changed some wording. We agreed to meet at the son-in-law's home at 11:00 a.m. the next day.

At the meeting on the day of the intervention, the RN told us that the identified person's condition had become medically more severe. I called the treatment center and told the intake person that we were going to take her to the hospital before bringing her for treatment. We went over the letters once again, the speaking order, said a prayer, and went to the home of the identified person.

The RN met us at the front door and took us into the living room. It was very dark; the windows were covered and no lights were on. The identified person was asleep on the sofa and needed help to get up. She was skinny as a rail. I asked the team to give her a little time, and to be gentle with her.

I usually tell people the seating arrangements, so I had the daughter who I thought would be my ally sit next to her. But when the daughter started talking, the poor lady, of course because she was three-quarters drunk, wasn't paying much attention to anything. A couple of others talked, and we still weren't reaching her.

They read the letters and weren't connecting with her. So I said to another daughter, "Why don't you go over to the couch and sit next to your mom? Ask your sister there to leave." She went over and sat next to her mom, and put her arm around her. Her mom started crying, and so did she. I think it might have been the first time in a long time that they touched one another. The daughter started talking to her about how much she cared about her, in spite of the fact that she'd not been around her. Tears streamed down the mother's face.

But the mother still said that she would not go to treatment, so I talked to her about my life, and also what effect excessive drinking has on our relationships with others and the human body. She asked many questions about my drinking life and my sober life. She finally agreed to go to the hospital and the family took her to detox, but she hadn't yet agreed to go to treatment.

Two days after she entered the detox unit at the hospital, the family called and asked if I would go and see her. She had changed her mind and wanted to talk to me again. Her two daughters and I talked to her about getting help.

As I held her hand and rubbed it and talked to her, you could tell it'd been a long time since her emotional needs had been met. She just needed someone she could trust.

I was worried that while she was in the hospital her husband would try to get hold of her, so one of the family members talked to the hospital staff. They said, "We'll tell the police and we won't let him in." She agreed to get treatment and went three days later.

Intervention Story: The Man in the Basement

Soon after I moved to Colorado, I went on a call for help with an alcoholic in the middle of the night. A woman answered the door and said the man was down in the basement. I asked, "Is he your husband?" She said, "No."

It was a true cellar without a concrete floor and no windows. Here was this poor man with hair all over, just a horrible mess, looked like a wild man. Bill and I talked to him for a few minutes.

I said to him, "Where do you live? Do you go upstairs?" He said no, they wouldn't let him come upstairs. I said, "Well, how do you eat?" He took me over to a bin of potatoes. He was living on raw potatoes, and he was just as crazy as a coon dog.

Bill hadn't been sober too long and said, "We've got to get out of here." But you can't leave a human being in this condition. So I said, "You help me. We'll put him in the car," and we took him to a crisis ward.

On the way, he told us that he'd go outside in the daytime. I don't know how he got the money to drink, but probably on the streets. When I see a drunk and he's absolutely desperate for something to drink and he asks me for $2 or something, I give it to him, because I don't want him to have to go through what I know he will. I give him some money and wonder, Is he really gonna buy food? But I figure my business is to give him some money. His business is what he does with it. I used to have to ask people for money many mornings during my darkest days as a miserable alcoholic.

Intervention Story: The Cost of Intervention

When the Betty Ford Clinic started their professional program, Bob Newton invited me to attend for the week, just as if I was in treatment with the others in the group. He knew that I did a lot of interventions, many of them on professionals.

The counselor who was the head of my group said to me, "Howie, the eight people that I have in my group are all professionals who have undergone interventions. Some of them numerous times. And they just despise interventionists and the intervention process. Bob Newton told me you'd be able to handle that." And I said, "We'll give it a shot anyway."

On the first day, she introduced me to them and said that I was an interventionist. Man, nobody would sit by me. They wouldn't even talk.

The second day it got easier, and then finally on the third day a doctor, probably in his early forties, came and sat by me. He said, "Howie, I'm sorry that the rest of the people in this group and I treated you the way we did."

"That's all right. I can deal with it," I said.

He said, "I want you to know, first of all, that I respect what you're doing. I have lost my wife and two children and a $250,000 a year profession. I've been in four residential treatment centers. I'm going to lose my license if I do not complete this treatment program and stay connected and sober and clean for five years. This is the best program I've ever been in. But you've got to have a little compassion for these men and women, because they were not treated well in their interventions."

"In what way?" I asked.

"Well, just about all of them had to pay for their own interventions. The interventionist asked for the money right at the intervention because he wouldn't be seeing them again. Do you do that?"

I said, "No, I'd never do that. All those arrangements are made before we ever do the intervention." He asked me to tell the group members that. The next day they came to me and said, "If we ever need an intervention again, we want you."

Intervention Story:
Complications from a Wrong Team Member

Once I got a call from a woman asking me to do an intervention on her mom, who had been drinking heavily for a long time. Family members for the potential team included the woman who called me, her father, her sister, and a young man who grew up with them. The husbands of the two sisters didn't want anything to do with the mom, and so weren't on the team.

At the team meeting each of the sisters said to their father, "Why don't you say to Mom that you love her? She desperately needs to hear that you love her."

He said, "I won't do it."

And the daughters as well as the friend said, "And you haven't done it for years and years."

He said, "I will not say that to that woman."

The daughter who called the intervention said, "Dad, if you would say that to her, she'd be much

123

more receptive to what we're trying to tell her."

And he said, "I told you, and I mean it, I will not say those words to your mother."

So I said to him, "If it's that important to her, why don't you say to her, 'I love you, but you don't think that I do because I never express it, because it's very difficult for me to express my love to someone who's intoxicated all the time.'"

And he said, "No, I won't even do that." So we went through the whole intervention and he would not say it. We must have been in the intervention two-and-a-half hours.

Finally one daughter gave a consequence, "Mom, I know that you love your grandson." He was a toddler. And she said, "Mom, you cannot be around him if you continue to drink. I just will not let you be around my son."

So the mom started to cry. And she said, "All right, all right, I'll go."

And I asked her, which I usually do, "Who do you want to take you to the treatment center?"

And she said, "I want my husband to take me, and my daughter. Maybe my husband will tell me on the way up that he loves me."

So they packed the bags, left, and got to the treatment center. The woman would not get out of the car unless her husband said that he loved her, but he would not do it. They stayed up there in the parking lot.

I've tried to figure out why his refusal was so great, and I assume that some things went on in that family that I don't know about. Surely verbal abuse, and some physical abuse that he admitted. I'm guessing sexual abuse, and in no way was he going to tell her he loved her. By withholding this he was probably saying that she deserved it.

I should not have included him on the team.

Intervention Story: After the Game

Once in an intervention with a high level executive, the team was the man's wife; a man who worked with him at his company, who knew him well and was in AA; three of the man's children; and a neighbor.

We went to his house to do the intervention, and at first he wasn't going to listen. We had to settle him down, and he didn't know what to think of me. So he said, "Well, I'm not going to sit in here and listen to all of you at once. I'll go with this guy." And that guy happened to be the guy who worked with him, and was himself recovering. He said, "We're going to take a little walk."

"I need to go with you," I said.

He looked at me and said, "You can go with me, but you're going to walk at least four paces behind me." So I did. We came back, and he did the same thing with a couple of other people.

Finally he said, "Now I'll talk to her." And I said, "And again, I need to go. And you need to understand something. I'm damn tired of walking behind you looking at your asses. I'm going to walk alongside you." And we did, and of course he was fine with that. He was kind of a hard-nosed guy.

He agreed to go to treatment that day. I said, "I'll take you."

He said, "Well, then you have to watch the second half of the CU basketball game with me."

We went out to the garage and he picked up his golf clubs, and leaned them against the trunk of my car. I thought, What the hell? Is he going to take golf clubs to the treatment center? No. I knew what he wanted. He wanted the neighbors to see them and think that he was going for a stint of golf instead of to treatment. And if I'd been real aggressive, we would have lost him.

PART SIX

Checklist for a Successful, Compassionate Intervention

Do

Treat the identified person with acknowledgement, acceptance and love.

Remember that this is still the person you have loved, but they are in great pain and they have needs that have not been met.

Research interventionists and treatment centers. Contact them and ask questions about availability, cost and methods they use.

Make all financial arrangements with the selected treatment center and the interventionist before the intervention.

Carefully select the intervention team based upon their relationship with the identified person and their knowledge of the addiction.

Be sure the interventionist spends time face-to-face training the team.

Request all members of the intervention team attend all of the training sessions with the interventionist.

Be sure the intervention team is united and has a positive, compassionate attitude.

Tell the interventionist if you suspect that the identified person will take his/her life, retaliate against the team, or if they are known to have weapons—any information that could make the intervention unsafe.

Choose a safe location for the intervention.

Write a letter of concern to read to the identified person at the intervention.

During the intervention, follow the speaking order and special instructions given by the interventionist.

Be sure your message is delivered in a way that will be receivable to the identified person.

Be honest with your words and emotions.

Be persistent. It may take more time than

anticipated before the identified person is willing to get help.

Create consequences that fit the situation.

Save the consequences unless they're absolutely necessary. Be prepared to follow through, no matter how difficult or painful.

Encourage the identified person to participate in a recovery group after treatment.

Don't

Do not tell the identified person you are planning an intervention.

Do not attempt to do an intervention without a trained interventionist and proper planning.

Do not proceed with the intervention if the team is wrong.

Do not lie to the identified person, except regarding the location of the intervention, if necessary.

Do not punish the identified person. Do not call him names or lash out at him in anger.

Do not get into side issues, like sexual abuse, at the time of the intervention.

Do not convey strong religious beliefs of team members during the intervention.

Do not believe everything the identified person tells you. Addiction leads to deception.

Do not give up hope.

I Stand at the Door

An Apologia for my Life
By Sam Shoemaker (from the Oxford Group)

I stand by the door.
I neither go too far in, nor stay too far out.
The door is the most important door in the world—
It is the door through which men walk when they find God.
There is no use my going way inside and staying there,
When so many are still outside and they, as much as I,
Crave to know where the door is.
And all that so many ever find
Is only the wall where the door ought to be.
They creep along the wall like blind men,
With outstretched, groping hands,
Feeling for a door, knowing there must be a door,
Yet they never find it.
So I stand by the door.

The most tremendous thing in the world
Is for men to find that door—the door to God.
The most important thing that any man can do
Is to take hold of one of those blind, groping hands
And put it on the latch—the latch that only clicks
And opens to the man's own touch.

Men die outside the door, as starving beggars die

On cold nights in cruel cities in the dead of winter.
Die for want of what is within their grasp.
They live on the other side of it—live because they have not found it.

Nothing else matters compared to helping them find it,
And open it, and walk in, and find Him.
So I stand by the door.

Go in great saints; go all the way in—
Go way down into the cavernous cellars,
And way up into the spacious attics.
It is a vast, roomy house, this house where God is.
Go into the deepest of hidden casements,
Of withdrawal, of silence, of sainthood.
Some must inhabit those inner rooms
And know the depths and heights of God,
And call outside to the rest of us how wonderful it is.
Sometimes I take a deeper look in.
Sometimes venture in a little farther,
But my place seems closer to the opening.
So I stand by the door.

There is another reason why I stand there.
Some people get part way in and become afraid
Lest God and the zeal of His house devour them;
For God is so very great and asks all of us.
And these people feel a cosmic claustrophobia
And want to get out. 'Let me out!' they cry.
And the people way inside only terrify them more.
Somebody must be by the door to tell them that they are spoiled.
For the old life, they have seen too much:
One taste of God and nothing but God will do any more.
Somebody must be watching for the frightened

Who seek to sneak out just where they came in,
To tell them how much better it is inside.
The people too far in do not see how near these are
To leaving—preoccupied with the wonder of it all.
Somebody must watch for those who have entered the door
But would like to run away. So for them too,
I stand by the door.

I admire the people who go way in.
But I wish they would not forget how it was
Before they got in. Then they would be able to help
The people who have not yet even found the door.
Or the people who want to run away again from God.
You can go in too deeply and stay in too long
And forget the people outside the door.
As for me, I shall take my old accustomed place,
Near enough to God to hear Him and know He is there,
But not so far from men as not to hear them,
And remember they are there too.

Where? Outside the door—
Thousands of them. Millions of them.
But—more important for me—
One of them, two of them, ten of them.
Whose hands I am intended to put on the latch.
So I shall stand by the door and wait
For those who seek it.

I had rather be a door-keeper
So I stand by the door.

Mary Beth Lagerborg has broad experience shaping books from topic development through interviewing, writing, publishing and marketing. She is the author of nine non-fiction books and a novel, and had served as a non-profit book brand manager. Her personal history business is Retelling: Creating Legacy Through Your Story. —www.retelling.net.

G. Dale Meyer, Ph.D has enjoyed a long career as a college professor at the University of Colorado Boulder and as a successful entrepreneur in both the private and nonprofit sectors.

He has received teaching and research awards, including the two highest awards at CU—Boulder.

His interest in young people has led him to create the Western Partners Worldwide (Wpw), which creates and implements mentoring and training programs for the world's unemployed young populations. He has developed a copyrighted process to mentor and train 18—30 age group populations to start their own small and medium-size businesses.

In his community Meyer counsels alcoholics and their families and friends. —www.gdalemeyer.com.

CPSIA information can be obtained at www.ICGtesting.com
Printed in the USA
LVOW12s0037070414

380522LV00003B/4/P